SUSAN MARION

Freeing Unconditional Love:

Unchaining Your True Self!

Susan Ann Marion

Freeing Unconditional Love: Unchaining Your True Self!
Copyright © 2010 Susan Marion
Cover Design by ClearView Press Inc.
Cover Art by © Irochka | Dreamstime.com
Editor: Michael Ray King

Marion, Susan, 1959 –
    Freeing Unconditional Love: Unchaining Your True Self!
160p. ill. cm.
ISBN 978-1-935795-95-7   ebook 978-1-935795-96-4
Self-help-Emotional I. Title.

126.1
Library of Congress Control Number: 2010936318

All rights reserved. No part of this book may be reproduced, stored in a retrieval system, or transmitted in any form or by any means, electronic, mechanical, photocopying, recording or otherwise without permission in writing from ClearView Press Inc.

Every effort has been made to ensure the accuracy and completeness of the information contained in this book. Neither the author nor the publisher assumes any responsibility for errors, inaccuracies, omissions or any inconsistency herein.

ClearView Press Inc.
PO Box 353431
Palm Coast, FL 32135-3431
www.clearviewpressinc.com

Printed in the United States of America

For my parents who really did do the best job with the information they had as did their parents before them and so on. Each generation improves on the last.

For my siblings and their families who taught me so much about myself
by being who they are.

And to all of my friends and acquaintances, past and present who blessed me with their wisdom, their love, and for sharing with me their joys and their sorrows.

Contents

Preface 1

Introduction 4

What Is Unconditional Love? 24

Where Do These Destructive Beliefs Originate?. . .29

Why Do We Have These Protective Devices? . . . 33

How Do We Create These OPD's In The First Place. 35

How Do We Know If An Old Incorrect Belief Is Activated? 39

What Do I Do With These Uncomfortable Feelings? 42

Feelings Are Not Painful 46

What Feelings Are There? 47

What Is The Purpose Of Feelings? 49

Part One: Exposing Your Destructive Beliefs 51

Massage 56

Affirmations 59

Conflicts and Irritations 61

Destructive Thinking Questionnaire (DTQ) 63

Alternative Behaviors 64

Resistance 67

Behavior pattern inventory 68

Daily Practices 72

Part Two: Challenging your Outdated
Protective Devices 74

Examining your beliefs 82

Part Three: Change 85

Creating your own affirmations 88

Part Four: Reprogramming yourself 90

A Final Word 92

Index 94

About the Author 115

Susan Ann Marion

www.FreeingUnconditionalLove.com

PREFACE

During my teens and twenties I suffered with my own addictions as well as self-hate. My friends at the time were also hateful of themselves. Many were in and out of prison, some evidenced symptoms of mood disorders and post-traumatic stress disorder.

In my thirties, I stopped my eating disorder as well as other vices. I went to treatment which gave me an introduction to 12 step programs. I started working as a counselor and over the next 15 + years I helped addicts, mentally ill and dually diagnosed who were often involved in prison systems.

This book is the culmination of my desire to help my clients, to understand my old friends, to understand why anyone would want to hurt anyone else, to understand and fix myself and most of all; I wanted to learn how to be happy. I didn't want happiness to be dependent on others or anything outside of myself.

The most important lesson I learned and now believe is there is no such thing as fact when it comes to mental health. All theories are beliefs no matter how we manipulate statistics to "prove" a theory. In regard to life or death, we only have beliefs that cannot be proven. For example;

Shawna believes when a person dies, they go on living as a spirit. This brings her peace and comfort so she doesn't live in fear of death. So far, her belief can't be proven, or disproved, but as long as she believes it, she feels comfortable with life. Will Shawna feel as comfortable with her belief when she is old and dying? If she is not, she may make a choice to believe something else.

John on the other hand, believes when you die, you die, you are no more and that is it, the end, finished. He doesn't particularly like that ending, but it is logical and it makes sense to him. It is comfortable to him. John's belief cannot be proven or disproved. Will John be as comfortable with his belief when he is old and dying? If he is not, he may make a choice to change his beliefs.

This applies to any beliefs we have about ourselves, our lives or about others. We have beliefs about everything, including whether the toilet paper goes in the holder over or under. The beliefs you hold about yourself and life are paramount to your happiness. Since beliefs cannot be proven either way, I suggest you choose beliefs that make you happy without harming others.

Why not harm others? Another belief I like is that we are all connected on a deep, unconscious level. Even if you don't believe that, remember anytime you say something to hurt another person, you are the FIRST person to hear it. Your unconscious mind has no way of knowing you are referring to another person. It thinks you are talking to yourself. It is a lose-lose proposition. The saying, "an eye for an eye" really has nothing to do with revenge. It is instantaneous. By intentionally harming another, I am doing harm to myself, my self-esteem, my sense of value, all in that moment. Every time I intentionally harm another person, I program this same information into my mind, under my awareness.

Conversely, I have found pointing out things I like about others reinforces these qualities in myself, or in uplifting another person I can't help but to uplift myself at that same moment. It feels wonderful and it is certainly a win-win situation.

As with everything in this book and in life, every choice we make has consequences, both pleasant and/or unpleasant. You decide which is which for you, then choose your path.

Freeing Unconditional Love

You are NOT a victim and you ARE in control of your life, even if you have made a choice to abdicate control to someone else. If you don't like that choice, make another one. While you cannot change anyone outside of yourself in order to change your situation for the better, you can change you and your beliefs. In so doing, others react differently to you. At first they will most likely resist your changes, but if you persist, they will rise to your changes, they may exit your life to find someone else to control or they may eject you from their proximity.

This book is one way to help you change the beliefs that detract from your happiness and to get to the life you want to live.

You are Unconditional Love at the core,

Susan.

Susan Ann Marion

INTRODUCTION
FREEING UNCONDITIONAL LOVE:
Unchaining Your True Self!

"I hate you, you're ugly, nobody likes you, you're a jerk, I wish you were dead!"

This horrible mantra played its recording in my head for years after hearing it almost daily throughout elementary school. Born highly sensitive to my environment, I struggled with loud noises; they hurt my ears. Confusion and crowds made my head spin and the emotions from others put out an energy I would often feel as a hail storm in my little body. Strong emotions from others in my proximity often overwhelmed and scared me to tears. My ready tears designated me as the "odd kid" earning a lot of taunting, ridicule, hail storms and more tears.

At first, I would come home and tell my parents school was awful and I wasn't going back. The other kids hated me." Some of the girls would pretend to be nice to me, get me to do demeaning things and then turn on me, laughing. Teachers hated me, everyone hated me.

My mother smiled. While she wasn't laughing at my distress, it appeared that way to me. I had determined my father wasn't very comfortable with his daughters, especially when they cried and he seldom had anything to say to me that wasn't superficial. I knew he would be of no help. My mother told me nobody hated me and to just wait and see, things would get better. A voice in my head said, "She's not going to stand up for me or protect me. She doesn't want to be bothered. I'm not important enough." There was no information readily available to the contrary. This was a logical, but incorrect conclusion of a child. There were many more to follow.

My mother probably had good intentions and she believed what she told me. Unfortunately, the taunting didn't stop throughout all of elementary school and at times it got worse. Toward the end of second grade, my teacher pulled me aside and told me she was at the end of her rope. She wanted to know what was wrong with me. Dumbfounded didn't begin to describe my reaction. My shoulders and eyebrows went up and then down. She went on to say she couldn't stand me and that she would not have me in her class another day. Visions of being kicked out of school and then my parents kicking me out of their home snaked their way into my head before she said I would be in another teacher's class. While I was relieved, now an adult admitted she hated me. When I told my mother about this, she looked angry. I thought she was angry with me. She may have called the school to have a meeting, but nothing changed and nothing more was said to me on the matter.

There was no one to turn to. At 8 years old, I had to protect myself with no knowledge of how to do so. How would I find a way to cope at school and find a way to become important to my parents so they wouldn't get rid of me for being such a bother? My fears and ensuing behaviors only brought on more hatred from my peers and teachers. I didn't know what I was doing wrong or how to stop it.

My three siblings were also unhappy for their own reasons. I was too self-absorbed to realize their pain. The older ones took out their unhappiness on younger ones and I was at the bottom of the food chain. My sister who was closest in age to me, often told me she hated me, she would hit me, sit on me and manipulate me. I would do my best to get her back, but she was bigger then me. When it was convenient, she would play with me. I was so lonely and hungry to be included in anything, but then she would turn on me in a heartbeat for no apparent reason. My parents had the idea it is best to let the children work things out themselves. I was completely alone because even I wasn't there for me. I concluded I could trust no one to be my friend without turning on me. If someone was nice to me, it was a ruse to upset me or hurt me.

Adding to my distress, one Saturday in November, when in third grade, I rode my bicycle up to the elementary school and played on the playground by myself. I noticed a man who was dressed like a custodian watching me from the bus dock. I was curious. He was about 23 years old and I had no one to talk to. I knew I shouldn't talk to him, but I wandered up to the bus dock and pretended I was reading one of the bulletin boards. He said I was very pretty and wanted to know if he could kiss me. I saw no harm in that. He wrapped his arms around me and French kissed me. I was thinking, "Wow, I'm grown up now. A man likes me." He asked me if I wanted a soda. I said yes. He directed me to his little custodian room, closed the door and kissed me again. He put his hands on my flat chest and I thought I was so grown up. Then he put his hands between my legs and massaged.

Out of no where, my father's face popped into my head with a look of disappointment. I backed up away from this pedophile and said, "My father would be mad, I have to go." The custodian probably couldn't chance neighbors close to the school hearing me if I screamed so he said I couldn't tell anyone because I'd get into big trouble: I did a very bad thing and my parents wouldn't want me any more if they ever found out. I already felt like I was on shaky ground with them. Forgetting the soda, I rushed out the door and jumped on my bicycle. The ride home gave me time to convince myself no one could know what I did and I'd go to my grave with this secret. By the time I got home, amnesia about the entire incident had gracefully set in.

The belief if anyone touched me in a way that felt good, I'd get into trouble or my parents would get rid of me stayed with me, but it was not in the forefront of my thoughts. It was a subtle, even sneaky, yet quite powerful conclusion.

During my twenties, I was sexually promiscuous, blunting my fears with alcohol. In my thirties, alcohol free, there were periods of sexual anorexia, 3 years at a time. While I felt lonely during these times, I also felt proud of myself as the picture of my father beaming with pride glowed in my head. It never occurred to me this was not realistic. My parents even told me they would be thrilled if I met a nice man and enjoyed a good relationship. The child in me believed they wanted to unload me onto someone else and not be bothered again. That child was quite confused and evidently, very much in control of my life.

For decades, anytime I thought someone didn't like me, no matter what the reason, I would feel the crushing pain from elementary school and of feeling so isolated. Anytime I'd make a good friend, within a year, I'd always do something to end it. I'd move away, make them angry with me or just stop contact. I didn't relate it to my childhood, I just felt forsaken and angry with myself because I thought I might be defective and bad. If I ended the friendships first, I was in control; they couldn't reject me and trigger pain. Just the thought of rejection by a friend made me cry. If someone became angry with me, I would cry, no matter how hard I fought the tears. If a man would be nice to me or thoughtful with intimacy, tears would flow like a fountain right over my embarrassment. I was victimizing myself with my own thoughts with no knowledge of how to stop it.

Why did I act like this in later years?

I never left those logical, but incorrect and emotionally charged conclusions about life I made during my formative years behind me. Those conclusions were the basis of my life interactions and the child in me thought she was protecting me. Since I thought I was on my own, the incorrect conclusions I made as a child were my only protection for decades because emotionally I never quite embraced adulthood. I'm not sure any of us do completely.

By embracing adulthood we live in the moment enabling us to pay attention to what is going on inside of us. When we pay attention to what we are feeling, we may begin unraveling incorrect conclusions from childhood. We step up to the plate to protect ourselves in a healthy manner using the organized, logical brain of the adult that helps us see when there is actual danger or just incorrect conclusions from the past. For actual eminent danger, there is an automatic protective device.

The way this automatic protective device works in the brain is if it perceives danger, it very quickly goes into what is called, fight or flight mode. This protective device is programmed to recognize sights, sounds, smells, feelings or tastes that are similar to what was experienced during a past perceived painful or dangerous situation. These particular sights, sounds, smells, feelings or tastes we'll refer to as triggers.

When the senses take in information from the outside world, they send the information to the brain. The brain filters it through a protective device; an automatic mechanism designed to protect the individual at all costs. If this protective device identifies a trigger from past danger, it then automatically notifies the brain to produce chemicals like adrenaline which shift the body into fight or flight. This can be done in a split second, and without our awareness.

Fight or flight is in the old part of the brain and it is automatic. The old brain is also known as the reptilian brain or the hindbrain. It is a piece of brain anatomy we share with reptiles and is the most primitive. All mammals have it and it is vital to survival. This automatic response works in concert with the protective device to push the start button. When activated, the body is flooded with adrenalin, the heart speeds up, digestion slows, muscles activate and blood is sent to arms and legs so the body may either fight its way out of danger or flee from it.

The reason that it happens so quickly and automatically, below our awareness is because in true danger situations, taking time to think can be fatal. For example, you are walking across a street with the green light and from the corner of your eye, you see a car swerving toward you and going too fast to stop in time. The protective device sees the danger and activates fight or flight (in this case, flight) and makes you run to get out of the way before you even know what was happening. If you had to stop and think about it, you might be under the car before you could give a conscious command to your body to move.

This protective device works for any perceived danger. The above example is a healthy use of this automatic protective device. Going into fight or flight when I think someone is rejecting me is like a familiar nightmare from the past that keeps me stuck in a repeating cycle of emotional self-destruction. The automatic protective device inside of us is designed to protect us at all costs for self-preservation. It appears it can unintentionally be misused. Because this device is located in the old part of the brain, beneath our awareness, it also doesn't know the difference between real and imagined dangers. It takes all threats seriously. This human automatic protective device gets programmed through repetition or through strong emotional reaction to an occurrence.

During summer break, before starting junior high, I remember making a decision. No one would ever hate me again because I had determined I would never be able to live through another 6 years like my elementary school torture. It was a powerful emotionally charged moment and I swore it would happen. My plan? I would become most agreeable to people who even remotely acknowledged my presence. No one would reject me again. That decision and the powerful emotions that accompanied were to determine the course of my life for the next 30 or so years.

Depending on who I was with, I acted as I thought they would like. I was a chameleon and so no one really knew me. Especially me. The only thing that mattered was, "Nobody could hate me." Nothing else mattered. The terrified child in me who was often in control saw this as a matter of life or death. I'm sure this behavior was annoying to most people after a short time. I thought I had to be what others wanted because I thought if they knew me, they would hate me: Hence my old childhood pain along with the familiar fight or flight would resurface. I believed someone hating me would kill me, just as I had programmed into my automatic protective device just prior to the start of seventh grade. My automatic protective device had become hyper-vigilant, often seeing evidence someone didn't like me even when none was present. It was like I was being blackmailed and I was both the perpetrator and the victim.

Throughout my teen years, in order to cope with this emotional blackmail, I began physically abusing myself with an eating disorder. It was private, I had total control over something in my life and it helped me to cope. With bulimia, overeating carbohydrates is followed by purging; usually via self-induced vomiting. I would over-eat things like pizza, cereal, chips or breads. Sweets are typical binge foods, but I didn't care for them much. Carbohydrates made me feel like I had a best friend by releasing serotonin, a neuro-transmitter, in my system. I was terrified of getting fat so I would then purge by sticking a finger down my throat. Other forms of purging could have been compulsive exercise or laxative use. Since I was compulsively lazy and forced bowel movements grossed me out, I stuck with purging. The purging behavior did traumatize my body creating a surge of endorphins, the body's own opiates. I knew this behavior was dangerous and not a sign of a well adjusted person, but it was the only way I knew how to cope.

In my twenties, I added alcohol, drugs and risk taking behaviors as a regular part of my repertoire of self abuse. The people with whom I chose to spend the bulk of my time were self-destructive, hateful-of-the-world types also, but exaggerated – they were my circus mirrors. You know, those mirrors that exaggerate our height, our weight and such. These mirrors exaggerated my self loathing for me to see. I was much smaller then my friends and much more sensitive so I would have died quickly had I taken my self-abuse to the depths that they were able.

These were people with good souls and big hearts who were even more afraid than I to let that loving part of themselves be visible. Instead, they were angry and all too willing to show anger to the world and to themselves. I considered it a joy, even exciting on the rare occasions when one or another of them would show me their vulnerable, caring side. It gave me hope that I too had this lovable part inside of me too.

Many of these people said they thought their anger was where they got their power. I gravitated to them because they were accepting of me and I knew where I stood at all times. I allowed these people to be my protectors, my surrogate parents, my identity. I became a rebel. I rebelled against authority, the government or anyone else my friends didn't like.

By age 29, I had earned my Master's degree and moved to Florida, closer to my family, away from most of the self-loathing people I knew. I became involved with a much less dangerous, yet still self-hateful man whom I would later marry. After a year of so called party time together, I got help for my eating disorder for fear I would die soon if I didn't. I sensed I was on the edge. We both stopped using alcohol and drugs as a result of my treatment: We both were ready to choose life. Whatever that meant.

Over the next year however, when I became extremely angry or frustrated (This man had a way of bringing this out in me), I would bang my head against the drywall or punch myself in the head. It was like I was attempting to shut off the mantra in my head through physical violence. Of course it didn't work.

One day when I was about 32, I was arguing with my then husband. He told me to "Shut up." I didn't respond well to that. The arguing escalated until it got to the point I was screaming in full drama-queen mode. He grabbed my arms and held me down on the floor to calm me down. He put his hand over my mouth as I was screaming rather loud (We did have neighbors). That triggered a past trauma and I went into full fight mode, total panic. I struggled with all my strength, unsuccessfully to free myself until I was worn out and exhausted. He asked if I was going to scream any more and I shook my head no. He removed his hand from my mouth, got up, went to bed and left me to myself.

I picked myself up and sat in a chair in the living room, bewildered and afraid. I felt so powerless and helpless and at fault for everything. I visualized and felt an impulse of me hitting my head against the tile wall in the bathroom with all my might. I realized I could kill or cause permanent brain injury to myself. I recognized it as a suicidal impulse so I grabbed onto my chair and decided I wouldn't allow myself to get up until the impulse passed.

That was my, *ah-hah* moment. It terrified me. I didn't want to die, but I was afraid of what I sensed was coming. The "F" word… Feelings. I decided I only wanted to be happy. I wanted to discover me, not the person I thought everyone else wanted me to be. I finally realized my chameleon tactic wasn't working yet I didn't know another way to live. I knew something had to change. I had to stop running from the feelings bubbling below the surface of my awareness.

I took a firm grasp of the chair under my body. I yelled in my mind to the feelings that were coming, "Give me your worst! I'm not moving from this spot until it's done" I started crying and shaking. I intuitively knew if I didn't resist the feelings and I didn't act on them, I would be ok. The shaking got worse. It felt as if a storm was raging in my body, yet, nothing actually felt like physical pain; just different and new sensations. I was both the experiencer and the observer.

After what seemed like hours, but was more like 15 or 20 minutes, the shaking and crying slowed until it stopped. The storm in my body was over and the sun was figuratively shining again. It was a new light, a brighter light so I could see things, as they say, "In a new light."

This was the beginning of the end of my self-hate. The clarity that came with this new light showed me I had been living an illusion: That I had never emotionally progressed past my elementary school years, thus, a child had been running my life throughout my twenties, a little less in my thirties and a lot less in my forties. While I had learned some adult skills, such as paying bills and keeping appointments, I had done that so others wouldn't hate me, so I wouldn't be dependent on someone or become homeless. It was time to begin growing up. It was time to protect myself from the frenetic child who'd been given a job to protect this adult with no possible way to effectively do it. My entire self worth had been dependent on the opinions of others. Not a safe or happy way to live.

I developed the techniques in this book to help me not only stop the abuse of myself, but also to accept myself unconditionally and therefore accept other people as well. It has been a hard road. I had 20 years of private self-destructive behaviors and publicly playing chameleon to get others to like me, a tactic that never worked. The process of discovering me has been well worth it. And you know what? I haven't finished.

I still have destructive beliefs and ideas running things undetected in my head, but it is much better than it was. The physical self-abuse has stopped completely and the verbal abuse is less frequent and much shorter in duration because I recognize and catch it mid-stream.

For the past 22 years, I have had no problem with eating. I don't even think about it. My body just tells me when it is hungry and when to stop and I listen. When it came to exercise, I didn't do it. My arms got tired just washing my hair. For the past fifteen years I have been working out and I'm in better shape at 50 than I ever was in my twenties. The thought of me using drugs is actually repulsive. Every so often, I'll have a glass of wine or other drink and then I don't want any more. It's freedom!

This book is not about instant results and it's not about becoming perfect. It's about learning how to Unconditionally Love *(if you don't like the word Love, use the word, Accept)* our selves one thought, one behavior, one belief at a time and that is a process. It's not the goal or getting the prize at the end, but it's all about the journey TO that prize that is the real prize: Experiencing bit by bit, feeling better, freer and much happier.

No one but me is going to fix me. Others can only serve as my mirrors to help me detect my problems. For that, I am most grateful. I am careful about allowing others to fix me. Sometimes it is a temptation, but I also know anyone I allow to save me from myself, I will resent. I must be the one to step up to the plate and fix myself. Others might be able to give me ideas and suggestions, they might teach me new skills, but it is all up to me to choose what skills and what suggestions to use and/or implement. No one can take the credit for my emotional health and no one can take the blame for my lack thereof. It is simply my responsibility to make my life as I want it to be.

When I give suggestions or advice to others, I need to listen because that advice is more for me than the person to whom I am giving it.

For so long, I really thought something was wrong with me. I was able to function in many life areas and I was able to hide my self-imposed torture most of the time. It typically just came out as low self-esteem like not caring for my hair. My style of dress lacked color and shape.

Now I dress in colors more suited to my complexion and while I still struggle between comfort and fashion, I come closer to fashion while maintaining comfort. My shoes were typically old sneakers. My make-up was almost non-existent. Then I wondered why people would judge me and I wondered why I was still so concerned with it. I still go through periods of no makeup, comfort only dressing styles and old sneakers. I know when this happens, I'm working on unearthing a hidden trigger.

Through the techniques in this book, I realized first I needed to accept myself. No matter my style of dress, no matter my hair arrangement, no matter my foot coverings. No matter my behaviors. None of that was who I am. Who I was and who I am at the core has never changed: Only the outer covering changes and if it changes, it was never who I really am. If I have to work at not allowing myself to change, then I am not who I think. Behaviors are only a result of my beliefs and my beliefs are not who I am.

After my twenties, living amongst angry, self-loathing individuals, I discovered something important. I still loved my angry friends, although I didn't always love their behaviors. I love who they were at the core and I saw that core very clearly in all of them. I saw the same things in my clients when I worked as a counselor.

If I could see this "loving core" in them, perhaps I had a similar core too. This book is my journey to get to my core and to live in it as much as possible: To shed more and more of my protective outer covering.

I have learned my core doesn't need protection. That was a bogus message I received from society. My core is my strongest part. My core, your core, everyone's core is UNCONDITIONAL LOVE! Yes, some people's core is so buried under destructive, hate-filled beliefs, they have forgotten it is there.

I originally wrote what follows in this book in 2001, but I kept finding excuses why I couldn't distribute it on a large basis.

I have since decided what I wrote is a system one may incorporate as they choose. I added forms and ideas to make it easier for people to learn and if they chose, follow the steps I took.

This system isn't magic, it's not a pill, it's not an elixir or liquid medicine., it's not even religious, although, you may incorporate your spirituality into this system if you choose.

Regarding the question, "Is it easy?" Our society has been after the easy fix, the effortless way to have the life of our dreams. What sells on the internet, on TV and radio are products that make your life easy and more convenient. Even surgery is popular because it gives instant results. Instant weight loss through pills, a miracle diet, a band or liposuction; the easy way to get out of debt; 5 simple ways to make millions. They don't take into account people's destructive beliefs that will sabotage them no matter how much money they spent on the "easy" method.

Do any of the methods work?

Of course they work for some people. These people have either made the decision to do whatever it takes and then they work at it until they earn the success they envisioned.

Or

The methods only work short term and then fail miserably through the person's own subconscious doing.

My own protective device thought financial success would bring people who might get jealous of my success and not like me or even want to harm me. I also feared taking on unknown responsibility that comes with success.

Most people want to feel good. The problem is they don't want to look at what is truly making them feel bad: They ether think A) it is something outside of themselves and say, "if I could just have more money." "If I could just get so and so out of my life." Or "if I could just meet the perfect mate." Or B) They sometimes take a short cut to feeling good through alcohol or drugs, overeating, serial relationships, sex addiction, compulsive cleaning or other distractions that amount to self-abuse. As many have discovered, that plan doesn't work for long and it has terrible consequences if used to cope.

There are no shortcuts. People often invent new ways to save time such as dishwashers, washing machines, and computers, with the intention of finding shortcuts to finish daily work. However, we immediately find something else we *have* to do that fills up the time saved.

Why? People often use being busy as a way to avoid looking at their own thinking: This is the true culprit, and the easiest thing to change (in comparison) once we know how.

Ever attempt to change someone else to make your life better? You'd have better luck in the long run and less energy expenditure if you got a shovel and a wheelbarrow and tried to move a mountain by yourself.

The ironic thing about all of it is the effort involved in truly making your life enjoyable is actually exciting, enlightening *and* it takes much less effort and has fewer consequences in the long run than any "quick fix."

The process doesn't have to be emotionally painful either. I personally detest pain of any kind. I have a low pain threshold. I already tried the *quick, easy,* self destructive route; trying to control others, buying the next promise to a quick fix. I can attest to the fact it certainly wasn't easy, it wasn't quick, it wasn't cheap and it wasn't effective at all. As a matter of fact, after 10 years of trying the quick fix route, I was in worse shape than when I started trying out quick fixes. Looking back, I worked harder at avoiding work on myself than I ever worked at actually working on myself.

Years ago, I heard a saying that hit home for me. I don't know where it originated:

"If I'm not the problem, there is no solution."

When I blamed others for my problems, I handed them my power to change myself. It was a ***no-win*** situation.

When it came to the destructive beliefs I held about myself, I was the problem in that I held on to them. As long as I chose the idea that I was not the problem, as long as I blamed those school mates in elementary school, as long as I blamed my parents or my siblings or anyone, it was hopeless.

Blame has no useful purpose. It matters not who I think is at fault. If something affects me and I don't like it, it is up to *me* to change something in me so something no longer holds power over me.

If I have a boss that picks at me and my work, she gives me a hard time and we have friction. If she makes my job more difficult, my solution is not to change her, but to change me so her picking no longer bothers me. This boss will soon lose interest in picking on me, I might begin to find it entertaining or she might even find a different job, but either way, I was the problem in that I allowed her to bother me and I therefore was the solution.

I change me by identifying my destructive beliefs, challenging them, changing them and reprogramming that part of my mind; my automatic, under the radar **Protective Device**.

What are destructive beliefs? I will discuss them more in this book. For now, I want to let you know what destructive beliefs do;

My destructive beliefs → negative thoughts → negative actions → negative results → so called proof of my destructive beliefs → more negative thoughts…

Often this cycle goes on under my awareness, but I am left with painful feelings. Because the thoughts seem so natural, I don't even notice them anymore. Not until I decided to bring them out into the light of my awareness.

Yes, for many years I didn't realize I had a choice. I had no knowledge I could even question these beliefs. And of course, lack of information up to this point was not a reason to continue to give away my power. I was thrilled to finally realize I was the problem: This was the only way I could ever become the solution!

Remember, blame is self-defeating and has no place in anyone's life. It doesn't change the fact if I wanted my life to change and get better, *I* would have to be responsible for doing so. No one could do it for me. **<u>I am the only one who can change me!</u>** If someone were to step in and make me feel better for a while, it would be a procrastinating gesture. I would always come back to my destructive beliefs and the need to become my solution.

Other people are helpful in that they are my mirrors. They help me to see me better and my feelings tell me when this is happening.

Yes, It would have been much easier if I had had this book and someone to coach me (just like everyone, I am often blind and deaf to my own beliefs so I needed someone to listen to me and point out what I was saying). It wasn't until years later when I was tired, depressed and feeling really beaten that I realized I could actually ask for help from friends and/or professionals. Unfortunately, I had destructive beliefs that said,

"No one cares"

"If I ask for help, people will see my weakness and then turn it on me to hurt me"

"I have to figure it all out myself or it doesn't mean anything"

"I had a Master's degree in counseling! How could I admit to being as confused and "messed-up" as I am?"

What did I mean by messed up? My beliefs told me many negative things:

"I'm ugly"
"I'm fat"
"I'm stupid"
"I don't know how to keep friends"
"I can't do anything right"
"I can't trust anyone"
"I'll never amount to anything."

Freeing Unconditional Love

> *"I'm F___ed up"*
> *"I'm unlovable"*
> *"I'm defective*
> *"With my luck…"*
> *"I have no choice"*
> *"(Others) did this to me"*
> I'd also ask myself, *"What is wrong with me?"*

and so on, ad-nauseam… Any of these sound familiar?

These days my destructive beliefs are much fewer in number and I catch them much faster so I don't have to be tortured (by my own thoughts) for very long and my actions are much kinder (No more self abuse). I control just how long I want or don't want to be emotionally tortured. It really is very liberating and the only things in my life I had to give up were:

> My self-identity as a victim,
> The entire concept of righteous indignation
> The idea I have control over anything other than my *own* thoughts, feelings and actions.

For instance, in my elementary school years, the reason I was considered different was I easily got overwhelmed by loud noise, confusion and emotional energy and I didn't understand any of it. The ensuing teasing often brought me to tears. I learned not to trust others because anyone might pretend to be my friend and then turn on me (as did happen a number of times); yet, I so craved a feeling I belonged somewhere, I would fall for it over and over.

I saw myself as a victim – a mindset that continued into my twenties. I would choose the wrong people to be my friends. People who would often turn on me and not want to be my friend any longer when I inadvertently said or did something they didn't like. I would always be dumbfounded because I only wanted to be accepted. It seemed easier to be the victim and feel righteous indignation over their deception and betrayal! Simultaneously I thought if I acted the right way, everyone would like me (I call it becoming the play-dough person). HA! It didn't work in the least! The best I got was nobody actually hated me because no one actually knew me. No one cared about me either.

Talk about a no-win situation for me. I repeated this play-dough person scenario (allowing others to shape me and become as they wanted until they became bored) many, many times throughout my childhood, teens, twenties thirties and into my forties. It was in my thirties when I made that decision. I wanted to be happy. I would not stop until I discovered the secret.

Am I happy *all* the time? No. Am I happy more than I'm unhappy? Yes! I always seem to have an underlying sense of joy, no matter what happens, even through depression. For many years during this process, I would become depressed. Although working out helped a great deal, I noticed if I didn't work on identifying my under the surface thoughts and beliefs, the depression made me miserable. As soon as I started the work as outlined in the following chapters, the depression lifted in direct proportion to my willingness to face my fears that were always illusions.

This system doesn't prevent things we don't like from happening, but it does make them easier to take. One of my favorite sayings I developed from using this system is, "Everything is in perfect order; even if I don't agree with or understand that order." This is a form of non-resistance.

Of course, when something happens I don't like, I do my best to change what I can. There are a lot of things I can't change.

My massage business had been off and on for years. For months, I'd be comfortable, putting money in savings and then there were leans months where I worried if I could pay the bills. I didn't start and run my business so it could be a success although that would have been nice. I started my business because of what it could and did teach me about myself. I liked what I became as a result of taking that risk. Each experience in my life changes me and gives me the opportunity to grow and be happier through discovering my incorrect beliefs about myself.

As long as I want to be happy, I will use my system. I have found in many instances, the things that have happened in the past I saw as loss or disappointment at the time, have turned out to be gifts of huge proportions.

I invite you into the system I have discovered. I'm sure I have not developed it in a vacuum, that there are other people, other systems that are quite similar. Choices and options are great. Where some people speak my language and have had similar beliefs, this book will speak to you. Others will get more from another system or book. I just implore you to never give up. Your happiness is up to you.

What is Unconditional Love?

I define Unconditional Love: To love others without limits or judgment; without conditions. It appears love is a type of energy.

So just how does one describe an energy? Now that's pretty difficult. It is easier to describe the results of energy. For example, no one even knows what electricity is, but we see examples of its uses every minute of every day in:

- our computers
- our lights
- Our (Electric) heat or air conditioning
- a refrigerator
- A radio or CD player
- The jolt of an electric fence
- In medical devices
- etc…

We don't even realize our dependence on electricity until a lightening storm blows a transformer and our power goes out.

All these are examples of the results of electricity. Love, like electricity, is energy. No one quite knows what it is and most likely we know more about how electricity works than we know about how love works. Electricity is easier to explain for most of us since it has a scientific foundation, whereas love has an emotional or feeling foundation. Feelings and emotions are traditionally more difficult to define, explain, learn about or understand.

We feel the **results** of love. We transform the energy of love into what we feel and what we do yet we don't really understand how it works. We just know it works because of how we feel!

Freeing Unconditional Love

From where does love come?

For those who are spiritually focused, one could say love comes from their belief in "God."

I would say love is what we *are*. We have the choice and the power to ignore or cover up what we are so we may experience misery and pain. The misery and pain isn't real, but it hurts just the same. Just like if a doctor says you have terminal cancer. The anguish you would most likely feel would hurt like you suddenly had no buffer against the world. The same thing might happen if you were told your mate lied to you or if you believed you would be fired from your secure job. Whether it was true or the news was in error, if you believe it, the pain is very real. Like that love feeling was suddenly cut off. The fact we might have cancer, our mate cheated, a coworker told us he heard we were going to be fired or other news is not what causes our pain: The belief it happened and the story we tell ourselves about it may cause us to cut off our love flow creating blockages so we experience what it is that we are not.

We could also choose to experience *more* of what we are and glow with love, happiness and the ability to live our life purpose here on Earth. To live one's life purpose is akin to Nirvana, heaven on Earth.

My choice is on the *more* side. Nirvana sounds good to me. The blockages are feelings we find uncomfortable, even painful. Having lived in those feelings for many years of my life, I don't recommend it as a habit.

Since we are never completely finished with uncovering destructive beliefs we will, at least on occasion, experience blockages to what we really are.

I for one am not into pain and discomfort. Since this work comes up at least periodically throughout life, I discovered one way to limit the discomfort or pain that comes with incorrect beliefs.

Non-Resistance

In other words, rather than resist what we think will be painful feelings, we need to embrace them, feel whatever comes and let them pass. We resist feelings by avoiding them. We avoid them through non-stop tasks, confusion, addictive TV or reading or self-abuse. Many times I would brace myself against the pain I thought would surely come, thinking this would lessen the pain. Rather than lessen the pain, resisting feelings is actually what causes the pain, not the feelings themselves.

The first time I embraced a feeling I thought would be painful, it was when I had the impulse to whack my head into the bathroom tile mentioned earlier. I realized it was either, kill myself or feel the feelings. I had placed myself into a life or death situation and thankfully, I chose life.

As I was holding on the chair to keep myself from going toward the bathroom, shaking and crying, I had the realization that it didn't actually hurt. It was fascinating. It was like I took a drug and the effects were just kicking in. I was like a reporter, observing and feeling the experience at the same time. I felt the shaking and the crying, but it didn't hurt!

After the shaking and crying stopped (about 10-20 minutes or maybe 5-10 minutes, hard to judge), I felt an amazing high. I had experienced not a lick of pain. Everything became clear. I realized what had pushed me to the brink of self destruction; beliefs I had developed about myself from a past trauma and their attached feelings. These had been triggered by my husband's hand over my mouth to keep me from screaming.

Since he had gone to bed, he was unaware of my life or death drama I had experienced in the chair. I flew into the bedroom and woke him up excited to tell him what had happened. I don't' know if he even cared to hear about it at 1:00 am. He was probably wondering what he had gotten himself into being married to me, but it didn't matter. I told him and I felt like I was floating on a cloud.

It doesn't have to be life or death. Now, I have a choice anytime a scary feeling is wanting to be felt, I sit down, and say in my head or out loud if I'm alone, "Come on, do your thing! Give me your worst." Or, I can resist the feeling and be unhappy, make myself ill, pull muscles, or lower my immune system until I stop resisting. It takes a great deal of energy to resist feelings. I believe this resistance also brings on depression.

The protective beliefs I mentioned above that came as a result of a trauma may also come as a result of an imagined trauma as well. In elementary school when I told my parents nobody liked me in school and I didn't want to go back, they ignored my plea and told me things would get better, I projected it would ***not*** get better. I felt they had no way of knowing how bad it was in school. I decided they didn't want to be bothered by my problems. I could foresee future trauma if I didn't protect myself. I foresaw I was on my own and at 8 years old, I didn't feel very confident. I developed beliefs about myself, about people, about life and about how to be safe.

As a result, I learned how to bury my feelings. I only showed the overflow and there was plenty of that too. I believed:

- "No one will like me if they get to know me so don't let them get close."
- "It is easier to make people hate me right away so they can't get close and then hurt me."
- "I don't fit in anywhere."
- "If I act as people want, they will have no choice but to like me or at least to not hate me."
- "If people just don't hate me, I can survive."
- "If someone hates me, they will hurt me. I must avoid this at all costs or I could die."

I wasn't fully aware of these beliefs, but they affected my behavior in many various situations. I had made it a point to not let anyone get to know me too well. Every so often, I would disappear and not call people to do things. Funny thing, they didn't call me either so I used that as proof they didn't like me.

I often would say things without thinking and others would feel insulted. I felt like a social klutz and sure people hated me and wouldn't try to be my friend. I figured it was ok because I didn't fit in anyway. I tried using the play-dough strategy, letting others mold me into what they want me to be. I knew if or when I said one wrong thing, they would reject me; keeping me on an emotional tightrope. That was my repertoire of coping skills for a long time.

Mind you, all this rubbish about people hating me was in my head and I made it real for me. I acted as if it were true and made it true for me. I don't think most people gave me a second thought. I was simply uninteresting because I was not real.

I had to use the *Freeing Unconditional Love System* to mine the above beliefs to the surface of my awareness. Once I had identified these beliefs and many more, I could go about the process of challenging them, changing them and reprogramming myself so they no longer controlled my life.

Where Do These Destructive Beliefs Originate?

The possibilities are endless. For example, when I was six or seven, my mother asked me to fold the laundry. She had folded laundry many times as I watched cartoons on TV, but no one had taken the time to show me the "correct" way to do it. She went out of the room and I spend the next half hour attempting to fold the laundry in a way I thought would make my mother proud.

When I was finished, the clothes didn't look as neat as when my mother did it, but it was the best I could do. When my mother returned, she saw the laundry and raved about what a wonderful job I had done. I enjoyed the praise and felt relieved since I wasn't sure it would be acceptable. When she was done complimenting me, I began watching TV again as she sat down next to the folded laundry behind me.

The next time I turned around, I saw my mother quietly refolding the clothes. I felt hurt and to make sense of what had just happened, I filled in the blanks of my understanding. My first conclusion was an immediate generalization of this situation to my entire life:

"I am incapable of doing things well."

Since she didn't bother showing me how to do it "right," I assumed:

"I'm not worth teaching."
"I must be too stupid for her to bother to teach me."
"I must be unimportant or she would take the time to teach me."
"My mother lies to me so she must not love me."

At that age, I didn't understand parents protecting their child's feelings, I didn't understand a less than perfect job, especially the first attempt, doesn't predict every future action and I especially didn't understand the real reason my mother praised my efforts. How would I have reacted if she **had** criticized me or yelled at me or otherwise overtly indicated I was less than perfect? Would the same belief pattern have been set in my mind? What if she praised my effort and then asked if I wanted to learn another way?

Throughout the rest of my childhood, teen years and young adulthood, I didn't trust people who said they loved me. I waited, looked for and always found the lie (often even if it wasn't really there) from the very people who said they loved me.

At any job I had, I always felt they were asking me to do jobs without telling me how they wanted it done. I would often say I knew how to do something when I wasn't sure and then complain to myself that training was poor. I often felt my work might just be a waste of time and someone might find out I was a fraud. While I worked hard at doing outstanding work, the slightest hint of dissatisfaction from a boss or supervisor brought on merciless self-berating and a desire to find another job. "Quit before I get fired" was my motto. I never held a job for more than two and-a-half years, but six to eight months was the average before I was looking for another job so I could give my notice. Years later I talked to some of those old bosses who said they were very surprised at my quitting as they had been very happy with my work.

For many years, any romantic relationship lasted no longer than six months. I often dated men with veracity challenges and although I would be the one ending the relationships, I would still be devastated and not date for again for years.

From this one example with the laundry, you can see how I created a lot of far-reaching and long-term complexity from a few mis-folded shirts and towels. We all do this in various ways. We seem to spend the first fifteen to twenty-five years of our lives creating protective beliefs or devices and the rest of our time untangling the webs of drama created when those beliefs become outdated, obsolete and destructive.

As a child, the horrible creatures I imagined hiding under my bed or in my closet late at night felt terrifying even though they didn't exist outside of my mind. Some of the information I believed about myself and about my world was just as terrifying as those imaginary creatures. These nightmarish beliefs were based on incorrect information about myself and I then created a world around me that mirrored the images in my head.

Old nightmarish, abusive beliefs or those that simply block us from our potential are held over from past experiences and situations that are no longer applicable to present day life. Perhaps they never were or we may continuously place ourselves in situations in attempts to prove those beliefs as false or to prove them as true.

I wanted very much to be able to find a way to prove those negative beliefs false. I thought if I could find proof I wasn't flawed or worse, then I could live my life much more happily and more peacefully.

On the other hand, I have found most people enjoy the feeling of being right about things. We develop a theory or a hypothesis and then we get a joy or a satisfaction out of coming up with proof we were right. Even if it hurts us.

For example, when I believed there was something wrong with me in elementary school due to my sensitivity to my surroundings, I had no idea I had continued to look for and find so-called proof I was flawed in adulthood. I did that through the use of drugs and alcohol and through spending my time with self-hateful people whom were looked at as they were flawed by society at large. This continued to prove to myself and to others I was right in my supposition. The more I incorrectly proved to myself I was right, the more I blocked my potential.

I had no idea I had a choice. I had to realize my old beliefs were outdated, obsolete and could never be proven as true or as false. I call these, OPD's or **Obsolete Protective Devices**.

Why Do We Have These Protective Devices?

OPD's are protective in nature in that they are designed to warn us of danger so we may go into fight or flight without thinking about it.

Edwin's father worked and was on the road a lot, leaving Edwin's mother, Cora home to take care of the house and the children in addition to holding down a part time job to help cover the bills. This was not the life Cora had envisioned for herself and she would often rage at Edwin, saying things like "shape up or I'll sell you to the circus." Edwin became fearful every time his mother became angry and always did his best to please her, not realizing her anger had nothing to do with him and not realizing she loved her son dearly and would never think of parting with him.

As an adult, Edwin would get into live-in relationships with women who were submissive and who seldom became angry. Edwin would do things to test his girlfriend's loyalty like going out with other women while at the same time, becoming very controlling, limiting her contact with other people, hitting her and continuously verbally abusing her to lower her resistance to his controlling ways. When the woman would protest, he would discount her concerns. When she eventually threatened to leave, he would violently beat her, threatening her life and/or her family. If she moved out anyway, he would stalk her and act repentant until he could convince her to move back in with him. Unless his pattern is interrupted, it could even lead to murder, suicide or both.

Josh also had an absent father and his mother acted similarly toward him as Edwin's. Josh married an emotionally abusive woman and no matter how much she told him he was useless and no matter how many times she would go out with other men, Josh stayed, trying to figure out how he could please her so she wouldn't leave him. He lived each day in terror she might abandon him. He knew she didn't love him and he knew he was getting nothing from the relationship, but he couldn't fathom the idea of her leaving him alone.

It's not the experience that determines our belief or how we will protect ourselves, but our perception of our experience. Edwin mimicked and accelerated his mother's abuse while Josh remained in the victim role.

How Do We Create These OPD's In The First Place?

There are a few factors involved here. The first is,

1. <u>Stages of Development</u>

As small children, we have minimal life experience and no ability to reason abstractly because a child's brain is not organized like an adult's brain. According to child development expert, Jean Piaget:

*The first stage of growth - **from birth to the appearance of language** is a period of sensori-motor intelligence during which the brain learns to work the voluntary systems of the body. The child learns how to focus on individual people, how to coordinate her fingers to pick up objects, how to feed herself and how to walk. At this stage, there is no ability to understand or think abstractly.*

*The next stage, **from ages two to eleven** begins organization of concrete operations, of categories, relations, and numbers. These stages are predictable and happen in sequence. The educational systems are designed around this progression in brain organization. At this stage there is limited ability to think abstractly.*

*The third stage, **from ages eleven or twelve to about thirteen or fourteen** is a period of formal operations. The child is now able to understand the logic of propositions, true abstract thinking and reasoning. In other words, he is now able to perform all adult mental tasks, although with limited life experience. The confusion of puberty leaves many opportunities to misunderstand experiences and to create incorrect beliefs or reinforce established ones.*

At all stages children experience both a survival instinct and an array of feelings, though they are not capable to understand their feelings in the first couple of stages.

2. Life Force

Sigmund Freud, founder of the Psychoanalytic School of Psychology, named the survival instinct *Eros*, the life force. Eros pushes each human being to stay alive, and to do this, each child creates a protective system of information.

3. Conclusions

As a child, you were like a sponge, soaking up all the information around you and organizing it to the best of your developmental ability, to protect you from anything that might harm you. As your brain developed, you were able to eliminate some conclusions such as the monsters hiding under the bed.

Others were not so obviously dismissed. For instance, you may have concluded if you were abandoned, you would not survive. This conclusion is quite common and brain organization does not so easily dismiss it, since it's typically one of your first conclusions and happens to be true during infancy and early childhood. It is a protective device. It is ***not*** true as an adult, but the belief system doesn't automatically change just because outside situations change.

You may recognize it as one of your incorrect beliefs that springs into action whenever someone leaves or even threatens to leave your life. People often react with terror or rage when they feel abandoned.

4. The World Revolves Around Me

During the first stage of brain organization, infants don't even know where they end and where anyone else begins. Babies seem to see themselves and everything around them as one, believing the world revolves around them and everything happens because of them, to them or for them. As they develop, children are able to discern separateness between themselves and their surroundings. They continue to see themselves as the center of their *universe* and they perceive themselves as powerful. For example, children commonly believe they cause their parents' divorce or a sibling's illness or even sometimes they are at fault for bad weather.

5. Fill In The Blanks

Adults speak in abstracts, even around children, thinking what children don't understand, they will ignore. Because children miss nothing, what they don't understand they translate into something meaningful to them no matter how incorrect. They draw conclusions that are logical, but due to the absence of vital information, frequently not true. They store these conclusions away in a portion of their minds, ready to protect the child if any similar stimuli appear in the future.

Some conclusions, even if incorrect, might spur us on to moments of personal greatness. For example: As a child I believed if I achieved something big, like the Nobel Peace Prize or at least acclaimed the best at something by the world, I would be loved and appreciated. So I worked very hard and although I didn't win the Nobel Peace Prize, I have accomplished a lot due to my strong wish to prove my belief true. Even if I had won the Nobel Peace Prize, it wouldn't have been enough to boost my self-worth and I seldom felt gratified when I did accomplish things. I tended rather to negate or at least downplay my accomplishments and I don't think I'm alone in this.

6. <u>The Child That Remains</u>

As adults, the child that we were still exists inside of us, with the same beliefs, the same limited brain capacities and the same pain. It becomes activated and runs the show when a familiar perceived danger or situation arises that the brain recognizes. (The good news is that when pleasant situations arise, that same child-like part of you comes out and you experience life with the same wonder and awe that you did as a child.)

How Do We Know If An Old, Incorrect Belief (aka Obsolete Protective Device, OPD) Is Activated?

The same mechanism that lets us feel the result of love also lets us know when we are being fooled by an incorrect belief that blocks the flow of our essence. That mechanism is: **FEELINGS.**

Feelings are the key to *Unconditional Love*. Feelings are what let us know *Unconditional Love* even exists. It is important to understand how feelings work and the role they play in our lives.

As a human being you most likely experience feelings as sensations in your body. Although feelings may seem to have a life of their own and can be overwhelming at times, feelings are merely chemical reactions that result from your thoughts about your perceptions.

Perceptions arise from your senses such as sight, sound, taste, touch and smell. Brain cells called neurons receive information from your various perceptions and send them through the Protective Device. If danger or pleasant information is determined, the neurons are instructed to create and send specific chemicals manufactured in the brain back into the body where they are experienced. *That* is what you feel in your body. You feel everything from panic, terror, an urge to fight or an urge to flee (aka: The fight or flight reaction) to joy, serenity, happiness (aka: love). There is no place other than in your body where you feel feelings.

Some people have learned to "numb out" and have developed the habit of cutting themselves off from feeling their feelings in their body as a learned form of protection. They either, through social pressure, know how they should feel or through just guessing, how they think they might feel.

For those who have numbed out either through addiction or a coping skill, the good news is you can learn to reconnect and feel again. I say good news because to feel numbed out might feel safer, but it is also like being the walking dead. One must do more and more stress inducing or death defying behaviors just to feel alive or else sink into the pit of depression.

In these busy and dramatic times many of us have forgotten that pleasant feelings are our natural state of being. In other words, our natural state is serenity, peace, joy (aka: love). Although many of us haven't experienced our natural state for a very long time, if at all, anyone *can* achieve this naturally pleasant state of being upon demand, even in the midst of a crisis if desired!

As you follow the ideas in this book you may experience various feelings as you uncover old beliefs. Some of these feelings will seem comfortable and some definitely won't. Feeling your feelings is more important than giving them a precise name. If you are afraid of being overwhelmed due to past traumas, there is something called ***Emotional Freedom Technique***. The website is **www.emofree.com**. Part of this technique is called the tearless trauma technique and it will save you from that overwhelm.

Our most common reaction to change and our most common uncomfortable feelings are the result of the mind's instinctive calling up of our fight or flight system. For many people change, aka the unknown, has an attached meaning that it is to be feared and danger could be lurking. Some people may react to fear with anger, sadness, helplessness or other uncomfortable feelings that are simply fight or flight.

Some people are actually hooked on the adrenaline that the flight or fight response releases into our system and associate flight or fight as pleasurable or even necessary. Do you try to squeeze in just one more thing before leaving for an appointment and then barely arrive on time or late? At work, do you promise to deliver more than you can? In relationships, do you often find yourself living out the same type of dramas? Do you routinely drive much faster than the speed limit or perhaps you go more towards the dare devil end of the spectrum? It might feel like exhilaration or it might feel like stress, but underneath its just old-fashioned flight or fight. People often do these things because they have learned to numb out and this is how they feel alive. Others have an incorrect idea that love requires pain or that love equals pain or drama.

There is nothing wrong with flight or fight, personal drama and doing things such as skydiving or other sports as long as you know that what you feel is a *choice* based on *your particular thoughts and beliefs*. There is nothing wrong with feeling any feelings as a result of an event or a thought as long as you know that it is your *choice*! YOU ARE IN CONTROL! (**NOTE**: Always determine first that there is no actual immediate life threatening danger. If not, the fight or flight response is a result of your thoughts.)

Susan Ann Marion

What Do I Do With These Uncomfortable Feelings?

Some people have learned to suppress fight or flight type feelings. Medicine, science and experience has shown that suppressed feelings can cause physical problems such as various aches and pains as well as more serious chronic diseases like high blood pressure, ulcers or worse.

Suppressed feelings can also bring with it emotional numbing. Emotional numbing allows us to get through difficult experiences without going in to shock due to intense emotional and/or physical pain.

For example, when I was twenty-one, I got myself into a dangerous situation. A friend of a friend got a trucker to give me a ride from college in Harrisburg, PA to visit my parents 250 miles away just outside of Philadelphia. When I met the trucker, my body screamed at me to not take the ride. I didn't trust my intuition at that time so I took the ride. A little over halfway to Philadelphia, the sun had gone down and the trucker pulled to the side of the highway. He reached under my seat and pulled out a briefcase. When he opened it, I saw handcuffs and a gun. He pulled out the gun and told me to get out of the truck. Without going into detail, he put the gun to my head and both humiliated and assaulted me. I stayed calm and just observed while going emotionally numb. When he was finished, he told me to climb back into the truck. He pulled out the briefcase, put the gun back in and slid it back under the seat. The driver drove to the next truck stop, parked, yawned and leaned over and fell asleep with his head on my lap. When I was sure he was asleep, I gently lifted his head off my lap and quietly climbed out of the truck. On my way down from the truck, I stopped when I saw the briefcase. I saw myself pulling out the briefcase, handcuffing the perpetrator to the seat and shooting him in the head. He didn't lock the case, he must have wanted me to do it. I had no feelings about it. I *stood there, half in and half out of the truck seeing myself shoot him over and over in my mind. I then heard a loud voice in my head, the voice of reason that said, "**Just go! Go now!**" I did as my conscience directed and while I was angry with myself for a few hours for not avenging my self, I am extremely grateful that I did not. I believe that had I panicked on the side of the highway, I would be dead rather than writing this book. I found a safe ride into Philadelphia where I caught a train to my home town. While walking to my parent's home, I gave myself amnesia about the entire incident.*

The problem occurs when the numbing continues past the trauma or the danger, and it becomes a regular coping skill. If that happens (as it did with me), eventually we feel emotionally dead. At that point, some of us use drama and thrill seeking to feel more alive. I may be stating the obvious, but I think this describes much of our culture today.

No matter how adept a person becomes at suppressing feelings, the body can only take so much of a bottleneck. For years, I used to stuff feelings and when it got to be too much, my body would spew anger, rage and sometimes tears, all without my permission. Some people may lose control, throw things, hit people or walls, harm or sabotage themselves or cause other sorts of damage. This outward expression of feelings is counter-productive because it validates the incorrect conclusions and intensifies the uncomfortable feelings later when the thoughts are triggered again.

Traditional psychotherapies often encourage people to let feelings out, to express them through techniques like hitting a pillow or yelling or screaming. While this approach brings temporary relief, I believe it also reinforces the idea that the underlying beliefs that caused the feelings are true. We feel justified, but still stuck.

If suppressing feelings **and** acting out feelings are counter-productive, what is left? The middle ground; what I call…

ACTING-IN

Sit down, breathe, hold on to your chair, place your focus on your physical sensations and simply *feel*. Dive into your feelings and immerse yourself in them. Remember that contrary to popular belief and years of societal programming, *feelings are **not** painful*. What is painful is *resistance* to feelings. Feelings cannot harm you. If they could, babies would never live through infancy. Outside of eating, sleeping and eliminating, feeling is what they do and they just don't hold back or block any feelings.

In older children and adults, health problems result from stuffing feelings or from acting them out irrationally, not from feeling them.

To just sit down and "feel" a feeling seems strange to a lot of people. But think back to the first time you drank alcohol or smoked marijuana or took a prescription or illicit mind-altering drug. You first ingested the substance and then waited to see what it would feel like.

*(NOTE: Some of these experiences felt awful, but some of these experiences felt incredible. The feel good experiences might be short cut previews to the feel good of **Unconditional Love**. Unfortunately, these short cuts soon lose their ability to take you to the feeling you want plus you get negative side effects or health compromises. Their purpose is to enable you to experience what you **can** feel, at any time, if you just learn how **Unconditional Love** works and then use that information.)*

You might have felt lightheaded, or spatial perceptions may have become confused. Your muscles may have felt energized or they may have felt as if they turned to jelly. With some experiences, you may have the most amazing feelings imaginable. If you never had any of these experiences, I don't recommend going out to try them.

A better reference point might be safer alternatives such as; spinning around and around then stopping, not eating for a time, not getting enough sleep or even the first time you engaged in sex or had an orgasm. All of these illustrate what you might expect when you allow yourself to feel feelings.

Most of us have experienced fight or flight when there was no actual physical danger nearby. If you try to resist the feelings, it can become painful or at least difficult.

If you would just sit with the uncomfortable flight or fight reaction, embrace the feelings fully by focusing on the bodily sensations without worrying about their meanings, just dive into the sensations, you may or may not begin crying or even shaking. You may temporarily experience a fluttery abdomen, tight shoulders, racing heartbeat, a sense of being overwhelmed or other strong sensations. I say to the feelings, "Give me your worst!" This speeds the process along and no pain is involved through non-resistance, just familiar sensations brought about in a different way. The tight muscles and upset abdomen feels noticeable, but with non-resistance and embracing the feelings, they are not painful. It is only in the resistance to feelings that you will ever feel pain.

Feelings Are Not Painful. It Is Only In The Resistance To Feelings That We Ever Feel Pain, Discomfort Or a Sense of Overload

Focus on your body and pay attention to the sensations without becoming the sensations. Instead, imagine you are a reporter, reporting on this new phenomenon without judgment. Tell your body to bring it on. Dive in. Embrace those feelings so that you may better report on them.

If you go all the way with the feelings, let them do their thing and don't resist, the feelings may seem scary for a few moments, but when they run their course (The less you resist, the faster the process) they will transform into what they truly are: A sense of love and reconnection with the world and with yourself. You will then feel a high greater than anything you may have experienced previously.

Once you experience this a few times, you'll realize that there is no pain involved or if you perceived pain through some resistance during the process, you forget it because you have given birth to a new experience, a transformation, a momentary realization of who you are because you have eliminated a blockage to that realization.

(NOTE: If you truly fear for your safety or in how you might react in physically feeling your feelings ask a professional familiar with **Emotional Freedom Technique (EFT)**. *If you just don't like feeling uncomfortable feelings, go to* **www.emofree.com** *and learn the technique yourself. Emotional Freedom Technique can help you eliminate any fears of feelings too.*

What Feelings Are There?

(When it comes to feelings, some people like to keep things simple and some people like to complicate everything)

There are basically two feelings. They are as follows:

- ➢ Comfortable, Pleasant Feelings
- ➢ Uncomfortable, Unpleasant Feelings

also known as:

- ➢ ***Unconditional Love***
  (Examples are: Joy, happiness, pleasure, elation, etc.)
- ➢ Fight or flight
  (Examples are: Fear, anger, frustration, hatred, etc.)

Funny thing is, the *same* feeling can be placed in different categories for different people. In order for a person to know what she is feeling, she needs to pay attention to the physical sensations. Feelings are felt in the body.

For example:

Fight or flight may be described as:

- Tight shoulders
- Increased heartbeat rate
- Tight stomach
- Uncontrolled shaking
- Shallow breathing
- Sudden increased energy

Depending on the beliefs, these feelings may be perceived as painful, scary or they may invoke a whole host of destructive behaviors.

These same sensations also may occur when one is feeling exhilaration as with thrill seeking behaviors such as sky diving, fast car driving, even some criminal behavior -- often described by some as enjoyable. This is all known as Fight or Flight, the ancient warning to us that danger is close or present.

While some people might describe sky diving as exhilarating and enjoyable, I would describe just the thought of doing such a thing as fearful and unpleasant. Some people find anger to be unpleasant while others find it enjoyable and powerful. Either way, it is still fight or flight with the same physical symptoms. There is nothing wrong with fight or flight as long as it is not the default state of being and as long you recognize it as a choice. Fight or flight takes much more energy and adds many stress hormones into the system that may do damage to the body over the long term if used continuously.

The pleasant feelings that go with love may be described as:

- Loose shoulders
- Lightness all over
- Sparkling Stomach
- Deep breathing
- Gradual increased energy
- Warmth inside

Some of the other words that are often used to describe these feelings could be happiness, peace, serenity, etc., but they are all **Unconditional Love**.

What is the Purpose of Feelings?

There is only one reason for feelings. They are your communication system with your body, your intuitive self and if you are spiritual, with your higher power.

When you are feeling *Unconditional Love* feelings (Not drug induced) that is your signal that says, atta girl! You just keep on thinking the way you're thinking.

When you are feeling fight or flight feelings, any of them, there are two possibilities:

1. There is danger or a threat of danger! (The legitimate purpose)
    - It may be a close call that just happened
    - It may be right in front of you
    - It may be imminent or unseen, so pay attention to your surroundings

(Anytime you feel fight or flight, always pay attention to your surroundings and assess for danger. Once you are confident that there is no danger, then go to the second possibility;

2. My thinking is not in my best interests and my intuitive self (and/or my Higher Power) is telling me, "Uh, excuse me, but your thinking is not in your best interests and you're going to feel like this until you change your thinking).

Feelings are not a result of you doing anything in particular or about anything happening in your life. Feelings are a result of what you *think* about what you are doing or what is happening in your life; your beliefs about yourself, life and how things work tend to be what drives the feelings.

YOUR BELIEFS → DETERMINE YOUR THOUGHTS → DETERMINE YOUR FEELINGS

Your beliefs drive your thoughts that drive your feelings so beliefs are a great place to start in order to get more of the above mentioned, atta girl's or atta boy's: to feel more of the delicious, exquisite feelings of *Unconditional Love*.

Beliefs have a major impact on what you think about anything. Your beliefs determine whether you will be a generally happy person or a generally miserable person. Beliefs that bring feelings of unnecessary fight or flight on a regular basis or even enjoyable fight or flight with the idea that it must be continuous (usually to hide from another belief that brings uncomfortable feelings), can bring a host of physical maladies as well as an unhappy, victim-like existence. This type of existence can become a repetitious pattern.

In order to change any pattern in your life, you must become aware of the destructive beliefs that drive the patterns.

PART ONE:

Exposing Your Destructive Beliefs

The first step in simplifying our emotional lives and unhooking destructive behaviors from our repertoire of protective devices is to expose our destructive, outmoded beliefs that I like to refer to as, **OPD's** (Or **Obsolete Protective Devices**). These OPD's run around in our unconscious minds much of the time, hidden from our consciousness, until they attack, telling us horrible lies about ourselves, pushing us into fight or flight.

It's not that our minds are working against us; it is because the protective devices have become automatic. The automatic part of our mind works much faster when any hint of danger is perceived so that we may act to protect and preserve ourselves without having to think.

The automatic part of our brain (Some people call it the subconscious mind or just part of the autonomic nervous system) has been programmed by us in the past through strong emotion or repetition so any beliefs programmed in, correct or not, are taken as truth. This part of the mind doesn't change without more programming through repetition or extremely strong emotion.

For example:

When I was little, I often heard my father saying, "If you were smart, you'd do it this way." I usually had never done anything the way he said. I also remember him speaking of some people he thought were stupid with disgust on his face. I came to the conclusion that if I were stupid, my Father would not like me and get rid of me, I told that to myself with the strong emotion of fear and repeated it many times.

As a small child, if I had been on my own, I believed I would die. In the eyes of a child, it is a life or death situation. My automatic protection device took this as truth and it never changed until I changed it with clear intent, a plan and a lot of repetition.

I went into fight or flight every time I thought someone intimated that I might be stupid. Since I had not been a fighting type, my fight or flight was messy and included leaky eyes, a lot of nasal mucus and a lot of swear words, but only when I was alone and those words were usually directed at myself. I was attempting to whip myself into shape so no one would know or think I was stupid. I wasn't sure if I was stupid or not, but I didn't want to find out. To that part of my mind, the possibility was just too frightening. It had been programmed by a child and accepted as truth the unfounded terrors of that child.

This happened for three decades and when I went into that fight or flight, I felt like a child. That is, until I identified it and completed the other three parts to this system: challenge it, change it and reprogram it.

The prime moment to expose our OPD's is when they begin their attacks. When OPD's step out of the shadows of our unconscious into the light—even if only for a moment—they're vulnerable to exposure. Exposure of OPD's is the first key to change.

If you are a Star Trek fan, OPD's are like the Romulan cloaking device. The Romulans had to uncloak their ship in order to attack and that was the only time they were vulnerable because the Enterprise could then see them.

There are many methods described in this book. Most of them are designed to get the OPD's to uncloak and attack so you are able to identify them. I offer suggestions. If you can think of your own ways to expose your OPD's, by all means, use them. All of the answers are inside of you. These suggestions are what worked for me. First I will list the methods and then explain each one.

Here are some ways to expose your OPD's:

- Log Book or OPD Journal
- Massage
- Affirmations
- Conflicts and Irritations
- Destructive Thinking Questionnaire
- Alternative Behaviors
- Resistance
- Behavior Pattern Inventory
- Stories
- Daily Practices

Keeping an OPD Journal

Keeping an OPD journal is an integral part of quickly and efficiently identifying your OPD's. Carry a small notebook or keep a piece of paper in your wallet or purse or start a computer file called, "My OPD's". This entire part of the system requires you to play detective.

These negative, self-defeating thoughts are running any area of your life that's not working as you would like. When you notice them and write them down, you've exposed them and can more objectively challenge them (the next key to change). You may either list them or describe them in complete sentences, whatever works best for you. Here are some examples from my original list:

"I'm Scared"
"Life is unfair."
"I'm stupid".

"People will hurt me if I am vulnerable."
"I'm useless"
"I can't do anything right."
"I can't trust anyone"
"Huh? I don't get it".
"I hate everything and everyone"
"I can't go on."
"Every time I try a new job or a new business or date a new person, my Father tells me why it won't work. I can never do enough to please him. Even when he's not around, I still hear him."

> **Funny thing with that last example, one of my daddy issues was that I only focused on the times in my life that I did not please my father. The many times that he was pleased with my accomplishments, I ignored or they just didn't seem to count. This happens because of that very human tendency that I mentioned earlier, the desire to be right or correct about something, even if it hurts us. I didn't have a belief that my father was pleased with me, only that he was not pleased.**

Paying attention to your thoughts, especially repetitive thoughts, can be quite enlightening, and you'll soon see how you may have been harming yourself. OPD's don't relish being exposed and will become more active. You have developed this elaborate belief system and it convinces you that the proof it has worked is that you are still alive. It neglects that quality of life is just as important as quantity.

> ***NOTE:*** *Remember that OPD's are simply old, incorrect beliefs that your automatic mind hasn't yet discarded. Your automatic mind has the job of protecting you from danger so it does what it thinks it must to protect you. It doesn't yet realize that it isn't helping you and it doesn't have new information. Getting updated information to the unconscious mind will be presented later in this process in the "Reprogram it" section.*

A number of OPD's may become quite repetitive or use so called logic in an attempt to push you into familiar, destructive action when you begin exposing them. This means that you are on the right path. Don't let these OPD's push you into anything. It is only necessary to write down each OPD once as you expose them, but if you keep a tally as OPD's repeat themselves, you'll soon be able to identify the most active ones.

You may be tempted to just keep track mentally, without writing them down. This seldom works. Putting them on paper makes a difference because the automatic mind is sneaky, bypassing the conscious mind to protect you. That is what it was designed to do.

Massage

If you want to tune in faster to OPD's as they work on you, you must pay more attention to your body and its sensations. Your OPD radar will become sharper as you increase your sense of body awareness. OPDs bring fearful messages and we often want to resist the accompanying feelings. The resistance brings physical sensations of pain or discomfort. A lot of us tune these out by becoming disconnected with our bodies, numbing out. This numbing out gives the OPD's and thus other people more power over your life.

It is important that you become more aware of body signals in order to connect them with various OPD's in various daily life situations. I recommend professional massage as a way of increasing your awareness of your body and the signals it is sending you. If you cannot afford regular massage, trade massages with a close friend or significant other or you can even massage yourself.

Massage is a natural action in human beings and other species. When you bump your arm or your neck is sore, the natural reaction is to rub it. When you pay attention to monkeys, they are always touching each other in a grooming ritual. This is also reassuring to the monkeys. Our society has made it **not** ok to touch others for fear that it might be construed as sexual. Massage is **not** sexual unless it is intended as such by the individuals. Non-sexual human touch is vital to our psychological well being and it also helps in many ways physically. For more information, go to: http://www6.miami.edu/touch-research.

Some things to be aware of in giving massage: Unless you have training in anatomy and physiology, don't apply a lot of pressure, don't apply any pressure to the front of the neck, in the arm pits, on the back of the knees and don't maintain pressure in any one of these areas or to the inner thighs as there are arteries there where you don't want to block blood flow. Get feedback from the person receiving the massage as to your pressure. On the abdomen, massage clockwise to complement digestion.

Slapping, beating, chopping or other forms of percussion are pleasurable with the right pressure. Just do not do this over the kidneys. They are on the back on either side of the backbone, just under the lowest floating ribs in the lower back. Pounding on the kidneys can be painful and may damage these organs.

Do **not** receive or give massage if you have alcohol or drugs in your system because massage releases toxins from the soft tissues for both the giver and the receiver. Having alcohol or drugs in your system at the same time is taxing on your internal filtering organs and besides, it defeats the purpose of reconnecting with your body.

Because massage is circulatory in nature, it is not recommended when the giver or receiver has a cold or flu or any other circulatory problem as you don't want to further spread a virus or bacteria through your system. This will exacerbate your symptoms and make it harder for your body to fight off the invaders. Avoid massaging around any cuts or sores. If you have been told that you have blood clots in your legs, light massage only on most of your body and avoid the legs altogether.

Massage is not recommended if you have uncontrolled high blood pressure because massage initially raises blood pressure before it lowers it so you don't want to risk stroke or heart attack.

People who have other health problems like cancer or diabetes or any number of other health conditions, should consult a doctor to determine if massage would be beneficial or not recommended in their particular case.

If you are in good health, massage that follows these suggestions can be highly beneficial in increasing body awareness as well as producing feelings of well being. You will be surprised if you browse through the touch-research link (**http://www6.miami.edu/touch-research**).

It is important to be able to pay attention to your body. Your feelings often result from your thoughts. Your thoughts, whether inside or outside of your awareness, produce changes in brain chemistry. The brain chemistry changes will come to your awareness in your body in the form of feelings. So massage helps you tune into your body and into your feelings faster. Do your best to make it a regular part of your life. You don't have to be a professional to give a wonderful massage. Just touching another human being in a caring, non-sexual way can be highly beneficial to both people and it is a natural act.

Affirmations

Another useful way to expose our OPD's is through a specific type of affirmations structured like this:

"I am _____". (brilliant, beautiful, funny, well liked, popular, tall enough, short enough, witty, creative, wealthy, successful, etc.)

On a separate piece of paper, define what each word means to you. For example, Successful might mean "has a family, a 4 bedroom house with a white picket fence" or it could mean "a world traveler who has lovers in each city they visit." Everyone has a different idea of what success is to them. Brilliant could mean "I am Nobel prize material who loves physics", "I am brilliant in my art work", or simply "I have a spouse and family."

Complete the sentence with words that describe talents that you have and/or words that describe what you want to be, even if it is not yet true. Create ten to 20 affirmations that describe every aspect of the wonderful person you envision or would like to envision in yourself.

Take three deep breaths and say them aloud to yourself, in front of a mirror. Look into your eyes as you say them and notice your internal and external reactions.

As you speak these affirmations, you may notice resistance in the form of negative thoughts and feelings, clearing your throat, stuttering and even repulsion. These negative thoughts may sound cruel and shaming. You may feel as if you're lying, but not to worry because you will soon learn that the affirmations are closer to the truth than you ever imagined.

The purpose here is not as much to convince you of anything, but to identify the OPD's that expose themselves to you in reaction to the affirmations. The mean, shaming, cruel, resistance thoughts are some of your OPD's. Capture them in your journal.

Conflicts and Irritations

You'll transform the way you think of conflicts with friends and family or perceived enemies when you realize these are another great way to identify and expose more OPD's. Whenever you find yourself in a conflict or recall a past conflict, first feel the feeling associated with this event. Don't skip over this part. By feeling these feelings, by acting in, you then see things much more clearly.

Things people say or do often will trigger your OPD's into action. We believe at some level that our OPD's speak the truth, and when someone triggers them, we feel threatened and flash into the fight or flight response. The stimulus causes us to believe that life will somehow be over if the OPD's are proved correct.

In reality, there is no reason to dislike someone who is not threatening your life or health. What we tend to dislike is how someone affects us. For the most powerful results, watch for patterns in your reactions to certain personalities and situations. It is not a matter of right and wrong. Just because you might find other people to agree that a person is wrong or disagreeable or just has no manners or tact, doesn't mean that you are not triggered and that you don't need to uncover your associated OPD.

For example: At a seminar, during a break, I was standing around with some women. I said something with a bit of humor and one of the women changed the subject with no acknowledgement that I had said anything. I felt that she subtly dismissed me with a look that left me feeling inferior. I had felt that I was part of this group of women and suddenly, this woman had turned everyone against me (All in my imagination). I decided I hated this woman. Some OPD's that were triggered for me:

- People are polite, but would rather I was not present
- I can't trust anyone
- I don't belong anywhere
- I am a fool, I always stick my foot in my mouth

My sense of humor is sometimes off the wall and that woman most likely didn't want to drag on an awkward moment. I doubt anyone other than me gave it a second thought. I felt those triggers the rest of the day and found it difficult to concentrate on the seminar. At the next break, the same women congregated and welcomed me in to the discussion, although I just stood there, pretending to listen wondering what they were thinking about me. The one I was really unjustifiably angry with was myself.

Sometimes people can be outright mean or at least rude. They might say that we are stupid or selfish or refer to us as a female canine or an illegitimate child using the "B" words. If the names that people call us angers us and there is no physical danger present, OPD's are triggered. For instance, if someone says that I'm selfish, I think that is ridiculous in some ways and in other ways, I believe it is good to take care of myself so I have more to give others. If someone said I was selfish, it would be like they walked up to me and said, "You are such a tree!" Of course I'm not a tree and of course I'm not selfish in a negative way. Both ideas are ridiculous. However, if I think that term might be true about me, I would most likely get defensive or angry and it would be time to write down some OPD's.

Destructive Thinking Questionnaire (DTQ)

Your gremlins and resulting coping behaviors tend to affect every area of life. The ***Destructive Thinking Questionnaire***, found in the Appendix, is to help you determine the extent of their influence and assist you in exposing some of your more prevalent OPD's. Simply answer the questions in the index to the best of your ability. Your honesty with yourself will ultimately clear your pain. Whenever you identify and expose an OPD, it will usually feel uncomfortable because the first reaction is usually resistance to change. Remember from the chapter on feelings, feelings are not painful and they cannot harm you. It's your resistance to feelings that causes pain and harm.

It's hard to believe that a mere thought can have such a powerful effect, isn't it? OPD's are usually the culprit behind our destructive compulsive habits such as drugs, overeating, repetitive dysfunctional relationships, smoking, etc. We're so used to them, they seem normal, but who wants to feel beaten up mercilessly on such a regular basis? We generally just sit and listen to their persistent droning as if they were the truth. By allowing them to do their damage unchallenged, we encourage them to control us. By fighting them, we also give up our "self" control. By exposing them, we set ourselves free.

Take as much time as you need to answer the questions - don't avoid them. Perhaps you'll want to create a special section for the answers in your journal. If you get stuck on a question, go on to the next one and return to the unanswered ones later.

Regardless of the OPD's that come up or the memories that arise, know that blame is not the game here and your past or current behaviors are not who you are.

Alternative Behaviors

Because OPD's and related behaviors affect just about every life area, I developed a list of alternative choices for you, based on the ***Destructive Behavior Questionnaire***. The suggestions are substitute, often healthier behaviors for the typical ways we handle life when driven by our OPD's. You may also come up with your own alternatives. Most people know on some level what changes will benefit them most.

With this option, choose one area with which to start. The object is ***not*** so much to get you to change the behaviors forever, but to identify and log the resistant thoughts to the changes, day by day. The OPD's abhor change and will fight to maintain its same old methods of protecting you. The resistant thoughts act as clues to your OPD's.

The exercise for this is also found in the index. I include the directions both here and in the index.

Directions

1. Choose the first area of life you want to change and call it area #1. I would recommend that you start with what feels like the least scary area so you can enjoy initial success that will set the tone for the rest of this process. Some people like to go for the scariest first. The choice is yours.

2. Begin incorporating the new behaviors on a daily basis until you have identified the OPD's you think are responsible in this area and you feel comfortable enough to tackle the next area. Apply new behaviors in the second area while you continue practicing area #1. If that is too much, just do one area at a time and don't worry about areas you just finished.

3. Continue this process with other areas until you have your list of OPD's. Take your time and be kind to yourself while you're doing this important work. This is something that you may come back to. There might be OPD's you miss the first time around.

4. Complete each area of change daily until you feel you've mastered the skills. Only then will you truly be able to choose whether you want to utilize the new way or go back to an old way. It's all about choices.

5. Some life areas will appear to be in working order. If so, you decide if you want to apply this process. Sometimes by attempting an area that you feel you have already mastered, by utilizing new choices, you may find a new approach works even better. This will open all sorts of possibilities for you as you realize that perhaps your approaches to life up until now have not been as efficient as they might have been or you might discover that you have a wonderful approach that you could share with others.

6. You will discover layers and layers of OPD's in this process. Write them down. This is a crucial step in exposure

7. Define any words that are not concrete (i.e., love, hate, stupid, smart, etc.) Many people assume they know what a word means, but different people have different definitions of abstract words. The more aware you become of your own definitions, the more likely you will expose your OPD's. By remaining vague, you miss them.

8. Review your OPD Journal each week and identify which beliefs are destructive or counter to your self-enhancement.

9. OPD's will sound logical and try to convince you, using your own logic, why change is not needed or why it is hurtful. Don't listen. None of the alternatives listed in the appendix are dangerous. Use common sense and get a support person to talk with about your fears. OPD's instigate the flight or fight response in order to maintain control. The thoughts may come in the form of yelling in your mind with reasons why you should not do this or that alternative behavior.

Resistance

If you find you are resistant to these exercises or to recognizing your OPD's, your resistance itself may hold a key to your OPD's. Which OPD's prevent you from doing the work or from exposing your thinking? I view OPD's as a defense system. Whenever you feel defensive, you are on the verge of discovering an OPD if you so choose.

Defensiveness starts in childhood, when our brains are not able to comprehend everything in our environment. As we grow, this system continues to build upon itself, regardless of the fact that what it builds upon is most likely incorrect due to lack of information or inability to comprehend. In addition, because its purpose is to protect, our defense system does not take kindly to being dismantled, as it believes its own incorrect conclusions about what is necessary for your survival.

Some people call this phenomenon the ego. When you change a behavior or bring to light a belief, the ego may feel as if your survival is being threatened and increase its resistance. You've probably felt this as a sudden rush of fear or anger that doesn't "make sense." This mechanism is not your enemy. It does not know it's running on incorrect information. The thoughts of resistance are only more OPD's that need to be exposed. Sometimes a deeper analysis of behavior patterns helps expose the ego's resistance. Sometimes exposing your OPD's helps to soften the resistance.

Note any OPD's that have emerged so far in reaction to this book.

Behavior Pattern Inventory

A behavior pattern inventory is highly effective in identifying your OPD's and maladaptive coping styles. The inventory is quite easy to understand and once begun, most people don't want to stop. You can conduct a behavior pattern inventory using a notebook or a computer. Handwriting often brings up more feelings than typing does, but not always.

On the first page, in the top left hand corner, write age 0-5. Skip a number of pages if using a notebook and on the next page in the same location, write age 6-10. Continue this process for ages 11-15, 16-20 and continue this in five-year increments until you reach your present age. Then on each page, make four columns. In the top of the first column, write, "persons involved" In the top of the second column, write, "incident". In the top of the third column write, "my reactions" and in the top of the last column write, "my OPD's".

Simply write about emotionally charged incidents that you remember during each age group, especially any incidents associated with fight or flight feelings. Most people don't remember much about their lives from birth to five years of age; however, you may have heard stories about yourself from your parents or other relatives. You may remember very little or nothing about your entire childhood, but I assure you, you have filled in the blanks somehow. Accuracy is not as important as are your perceptions for it is your perceptions that have been the basis of your OPD's. If you can think of nothing for a category, make stuff up. Your unconscious mind will most likely give you clues to your OPD's in your fiction.

Ages 6-10 *Example:*

Persons involved	Incident	My Reactions	My OPD's
Mom	*She slapped my face for using a swear word, even though I didn't know what it meant.*	*I cried, stormed into my room and threw things across the room. I broke prized possessions that mom had given to me.*	*It's bad to experiment. I'm not worth listening to for an explanation. My mother hates me. She might get rid of me. People pretend to love me and then turn on me.*

Under "persons involved," you don't have to include yourself as you will be in every incident. It is implied by the exercise. Of course, you may write that you are involved if you like.

Under "incidents", you don't have to write a long essay about the incident. Here you are simply writing reminder words for *you* so you may remember to what you are referring.

As you write, the "reaction" column will begin to reveal patterns of behavior throughout your life. As in the "incident" column, it's not necessary to write an essay. Just write enough so you remind yourself of your reactions when you go back and read the inventory.

You may hold off on the "OPD" Column until you are finished writing about incidents for the day or you may try to uncover them as you go. You may wait until you complete your first round of this inventory and then go back to play detective and figure out possible OPD's. As always, it is up to you as to what you think works best for you.

This exercise is exciting and fascinating in that it will allow you to be an observer of yourself. There is nothing to feel bad about, regardless of your past behavior. Any less-than-desirable behaviors have resulted from incorrect conclusions about your self. Those behaviors are ***not*** who you are. Anyone who had developed your logical conclusions based on your personal experiences would have reacted in a similar way as did you. Remember to be kind to yourself. You haven't met the real you yet. I guarantee that when you do met the real you, you will be quite pleased. If you are not pleased, you haven't yet met the real you. How simple is that?

Stories

People often tell stories about themselves and about their past. No doubt, you have your own stories. Pay attention to what you repeatedly tell yourself or other people. Begin to write these down.

Example:

"I just don't seem to be able to do anything right. When I was 17 I was trying to act cool in front of a guy I liked and demurely sauntered by him. Because I was looking his way to make sure he was looking at me, I walked smack into a bush and fell face forward. My pride was hurt more than anything. I have been making a fool of myself ever since."

OR

"I never accomplished anything worthwhile. No matter what I do, it is never good enough. I never seem to be able to get ahead financially. I put a little money away, the bottom falls out and a big bill comes along to wipe me out. I live month to month and some months I just barely squeak by. I'm such a failure. .

We all have our stories. Some of them are funny and some are tragic. A lot of them are complaints disguised as stories. People often get into telling stories about who had it worse in the past or who suffers the most in the present. These types of stories usually get told over and over to ourselves only or to different people, and we seldom tire of telling them. We think they're either entertaining or we just don't even realize what we're doing. Write out these stories. They also contain OPD's. Our stories can be one liners too. There is a longer story behind the one liners.

Clues to stories are one liners such as, *"This is who (or the way) I am"* or *"I always..."*

Can you guess what the OPD's to the above stories are?

1.
- I can't do anything right
- I'm a klutz
- I'm a fool
- I'll never attract a man I want

2.
- I'm a failure
- I'm worthless
- I have bad luck
- The world hates me, it doesn't want me to succeed

Daily Practices

As you create a daily routine that supports your health and well being, you'll find OPD's interfere. They might tell you you're too tired to say your evening prayers if that is important to you, even though you always feel better when you do them. Your OPD's might tell you you're too tired to go to the gym or do your exercise even though you always feel much better after you exercise. OPD's might tell you that flossing or brushing your teeth is so mundane and you have better things to do even though you have suffered from having to fix poor dental hygiene in the past.

Pay attention to your daily routine. Decide what parts are beneficial to you and which ones need to go. For example, in my twenties, my morning routine was to empty my bladder, take a shower, get dressed, brush my teeth, eat breakfast, play computer or watch TV and go to work. I kept most of my morning routine except for the computer/TV and I instead added exercise. My OPD's told me, "You deserve to goof off before work; you don't get to goof off at work, its important to chill. Who needs exercise? It isn't fun, lots of people go through life without exercising. Why do I have to exercise and they don't?"

My OPD's were attempting to keep things status quo. If I started exercising in the morning, I might feel better and I'd be more likely to make more changes. By keeping the status quo, I could continue feeling badly about myself for being out of shape and wasting my mind on TV or internet drivel. With exercise, I'd be more likely to want to write, one of my favorite hobbies that I don't allow myself when I'm am buying into my OPD's. OPD's hate change.

As you go about your day, listen to the types of things you say automatically when you do something. Pay attention to the comments others repeatedly make to you and your internal commentaries in response. Make lists of your goals, desires and fears to expose the sarcastic remarks of your OPD's.

OPD's are the creations of a child so they are obvious when you are looking for them. They sound like chatter and not friendly chatter either. Doing the exercises in this book with a friend will also help you identify recurring themes and they can point out things that you might otherwise miss. Notice any resistance or negative self-talk and capture those OPD's on paper.

For the first few days, this chatter inside my head would go on for hours with brief respites only when I focused on something else that needed my attention. I learned that when the chatter starts, to just write them down and then just observe without giving any energy to them. While identifying my tormentors took away their power over me, they were still annoying and very persistent. Identifying wasn't enough. It was only the first part of the process. When I went on to the next part of this process, I found that I gave them less power over me.

PART TWO:

Challenging Your OPD's

You've done a great job of learning so many ways to expose your OPD's and capturing them onto paper and into your consciousness. It's now time to take their power away. We do that by:

- Learning to parent ourselves.
- Examining our beliefs that have become our OPD's, in minute detail

Parenting Yourself

As children, we do not typically know when enough is enough. We don't know how to set limits or look into the future to imagine consequences or to know the value of delayed gratification.

People with self-destructive behaviors have a tendency to not trust themselves. Why? People who engage in self-destructive or self-sabotaging behaviors do not like themselves, at least in one area of their lives. When you like someone, you tend to behave in a supportive way and want to enhance that person's existence, not destroy their health, their self-esteem or sabotage them.

To intentionally set out to destroy someone's health, self esteem or sabotage them is a form of abuse. It must be learned or developed through OPD's. In other words, if this form of abuse is learned, it is usually from a parent, teacher or some other guardian that is important in the life of the child. The guardian may demonstrate this on the child outright through neglect or emotional, mental, physical or sexual abuse or the guardian might be quite kind and loving to the child, but abusive or at least neglectful to themselves in some way(s).

Of all the types of abuse, the worst and most lasting abuse is the kind that you mete out to yourself as an adult. You most likely abuse yourself as a result of your incorrect conclusions about yourself, which originated in childhood. This child has had to be in charge, take things into his own hands to ensure survival because he has determined that no one else will be there for him.

In addition, this child is waiting for an adequate adult to come along and parent him. It has been a fantasy to have this wonderful parent come along and make him feel safe and teach him what he needs to know in order to maneuver through life successfully. This child inside each of us looks to others to parent him. He looks to mates, bosses, the government, anyone that will help him to set limits and make him feel safe. At the same time, he will test these individuals for consistency and to make sure they are the person for whom he wished.

He may go through a number of individuals for most will fall short, failing his rigorous testing. He may finally find someone who is very strict, bossy and consistent. He might feel, at last, he as found someone to make him feel safe so he may once again be a child and have fun without worrying because this person will protect him from himself. It won't take long, however, until he resents this individual for being the very thing he thought he wanted and needed.

Why?

Because once we turn 18, we legally become an adult in this society. It is too late for someone else to parent us because anyone else will always fall short, we will come to resent these people because *we* must step up to the plate and begin to parent ourselves.

Imagine a child who's in charge of an adult. In families where the parents are alcoholics or drug abusers or otherwise

emotionally unavailable, the child often must take the adult role, nursing the parents when they are hung over, taking care of siblings, worrying about paying bills, and cooking meals. Even in less extreme scenarios, if the child concludes (accurately or not) that he cannot trust his parents, he may live and act as if he is on his own for the rest of his life with the same persistent child-like fears. This may happen regardless of the intentions or skills of the parents.

You may think that you were not adequately parented. As you look to your past, you may conclude that you were not taught enough about life by your parent(s) or you might think that you were not loved enough or that adulthood was forced upon you at a young age because of what you saw as inadequacies in your parents. You may feel that your parents were very loving and gave you everything you needed as a child, but perhaps they didn't give these things to themselves. Perhaps they didn't model self-care and self-esteem. You may remember your childhood as being wonderful and that your parents were ideal. Perhaps a teacher, school bullies or neighbors helped you to form incorrect conclusions about yourself leaving you with your OPD's. Even in this case, the child was feeling unprotected. Some of these memories may be accurate and some won't be easy to prove, but again, it is the perception that determines the conclusions a child draws. This is not a blame game. Whether your parents were saints or monsters or anything in-between is not the issue. Many of us are still looking to be adequately parented. Perhaps your parents did such a good job, that you wanted it to continue and failed to step into the role for yourself. There seems to be a consistent fantasy that, "If only I had that ideal parent, I could have had a happy life as a capable, successful adult." Rather than stepping into that role for ourselves, we look to others to parent us in an attempt to make up for what we think we missed in childhood.

To find someone to play this role for us, we often act as out-of-control children in various areas of our lives in an attempt to manipulate others into playing the parent role.

Self-destructive acting out is often a cry for a loving parent to set limits and make you feel safe. Addictions such as alcoholism are an example of this. Drinking too much alcohol is like a child getting a hold of the icing bowl or the cookie jar to enjoy as much as she wants of the treat. She doesn't know if she will get any again in the near future so she consumes as much as she can. If no parent is near to stop her, she will overeat until she can't eat anymore, she will get all wound up and run around like a banshee until she runs out of energy or she will eat until she feels sick. She then wonders why a parent didn't stop her; protect her from herself. Alcohol is the grown up version of the cookie jar. If the parent continues to fill the cookie jar, even though the child got horribly sick last time, she will usually repeat the process over and over enjoying the sugar buzz or the serotonin buzz, each time hoping that someone will stop her and protect her from herself.

You may look to a romantic partner or a boss. Some people even look to the government to parent them, living a lifetime on welfare or in jails or institutions. The truth is, once a person turns 18, it's truly too late for anyone else to parent them. Even if by some wild miracle, your parents (or guardians) suddenly became everything you might have wished for, you would not trust them and would begin resenting them.

If you found a spouse who was willing and able to parent you as you may have wished, after a while, you would come to resent that person. After age eighteen, it **has** to come from you. *You* must begin the task of becoming your own parent.

***How*?**

First you make a list of all the qualities you have ever wanted in an ideal, perfect parent. Think of any qualities you enjoyed in your own parents or guardians; imagine qualities you have dreamed would have made life better had your parents or guardians practiced them; think of qualities you've seen demonstrated in friend's parents or in TV families. Go to the library or bookstore and find books on parenting to get ideas. Ask friends what qualities they would have wanted in a perfect parent. If any of your friends' ideas resonate with you, add them to your list. Be specific. Rather than say, "Shows me that they love me," list the specific things perfect parents might do to show you that they love you. If you find yourself saying, "I have no idea how to parent myself or anyone else!" that might be an OPD trying to discourage you. You *do* have good ideas in this matter. Write them down. If you still don't know, act as if you did know. Play pretend. If you have a child, what kind of parent do you want to be for your child? Look at what you see as your own shortcomings as a parent and put qualities you would like to have had. Learning to parent yourself is the greatest gift you can give to your child.

Some examples of qualities of a **Perfect Parent** might include:

> *Understands me and my feelings, encourages me to talk, and doesn't give up*
> *Listens to me*
> *Buys me fun things*
> *Explains things to me*
> *Helps me learn from my mistakes*
> *Smart*
> *Happy*
> *Spends time with me*
> *Encouraging*
> *Patient*

Loves me no matter what
Teaches me how to use money wisely
Encourages me to discover my talents and my life's work
Allows me to be me, accepts all of me.
Protects me
Sets limits
Is consistent

Your list will most likely be similar to the qualities you might want in a ***loving higher power***, your "God."

A leader can get compliance from followers or underlings through fear and intimidation, but that compliance only happens as long as the feared one's presence is felt.

Conversely, when a leader leads through love, kindness, understanding and clear boundaries, that leader generates devotion from his followers. An ideal parent is no different.

Up to this point, you may have parented yourself through fear and intimidation. This often involves abuse, both verbal and physical. The physical abuse may look like addictions, destructive relationships and even self-mutilation. Verbal abuse manifests as the OPD's and the associated feelings with the intention, *"It keeps me in line."* The goal of this section is to enable you to begin developing the qualities written on your ***perfect parent*** list toward the child inside of you.

Your parents may have treated you extremely well, but if they neglected/abused themselves then you probably learned to neglect/abuse your self.

Part of you is most likely still thinking like a child. Your incorrect conclusions are from your childhood and built upon throughout life. That child part of you is the one who has been trying to parent you, but it lacks the skills and information you need. Your *perfect parent* list is your model. I encourage you to practice using these qualities towards yourself. For instance, telling yourself all the things you wanted to hear from your own parents. Next time your OPD's come up and start tormenting you, step in as a loving parent and challenge them, comfort that scared part of your thinking.

How?

When An OPD such as, "I am worthless" becomes active, rather than reacting with fear, anger or self-abuse, I suggest you begin talking to yourself as that loving parent in your list. Comfort yourself as you would have wanted to be comforted as a child. Explain to yourself (as you might for your own child or a nephew or niece) why the idea that you are worthless couldn't possibly be true.

Caress your head or hands or give yourself a hug. You now know, as an adult, what you would have wanted to hear and now you are in full control of the interaction. Many people find many ways to do this for their own children or even children they hardly know, but still refuse to do so for themselves. It is of utmost importance to do this for your self.

If you have children, they need the model of adults who are able to parent themselves. Otherwise, they will be searching for someone to do the job for them for the rest of their lives. That only leads to disappointment, torn relationships and/or poor work relationships—and more destructive behavior.

As you comfort yourself and develop your self-parenting skills, you will also be challenging your OPD's. The purpose of this step is to challenge these incorrect belief systems. As you do this work, more OPD's will appear as if they heard a new parent is in town and they are waiting in line, to be exposed, written down and challenged.

Destructive OPD's don't' want to destroy you. They just don't know how else to do their job. Although challenging your OPD's doesn't feel great at first, I encourage you to continue. It will soon begin to feel good because you'll realize that as you expose and challenge each OPD, they begin to lose their power over your feelings and your behavior. You must learn to depend on yourself for the parenting you crave.

Continue recording on paper your OPD's as they fight to maintain control and to test your resolve at parenting yourself. Having support people in your life is helpful, but if you begin to utilize them as your surrogate parent, you will create resentments and disappointments and additional OPD's.

Challenges to OPD's will sound like an ideal parent soothing a frightened child. When your OPD's are triggered, comfort yourself as you would want to do for a child you love or care for.

Just as it would not be prudent to argue with a child, it's important that you not argue with your OPD's. By arguing, you give them energy and power in your mind. Instead, parent yourself with loving firmness. Listen for the fears and acknowledge them before correcting them. If you are at a loss at how to comfort yourself, ask someone you consider a good parent what she or he might say to a child with a specific OPD you have then decide which words are right for you.

Examining Your Beliefs

Once you have a list of OPD's, I suggest you ask yourself some questions. My very long original list of OPD's included:

- *I'm incapable of doing anything right*
- *I'm worthless*
- *Trust no one*
- *I'm unlovable*

Choose the OPD's you want to work on first. Pick 1 or 2 to start. Ask yourself about your identified OPD: "If this belief were somehow proven true beyond any doubt, what might happen to me?"

What might happen to someone who:
- *Can't do anything right?*
- *Is worthless?*
- *Can trust no one?*
- *Is unlovable?*

For the first question, what might happen to a person who can't do anything right, the answer might be,
- *He or she wouldn't be able to hold a job.*

Then ask the question,
- *What might happen to a person who cannot hold a job?*

The answers might be,
- *He or she would probably end up on the streets.*
- *Someone that has ended up on the streets is looked down upon*
- *Someone who is looked down upon usually looses any sense of worth*

- *Someone who looses a sense of worth has to either steal or fight to get food and basic needs met.*
- *People who have to steal or fight to get food and basic needs met will eventually meet up with someone who is stronger or smarter and will get beaten up.*
- *People who get beaten up have to find others for protection and the only other people who will accept a street person is another street person.*
- *In order to be a street person, one must use drugs and/or alcohol*
- *Drug addicts or alcoholics usually end up dead or worse.*

The idea is to keep asking the, "what-might-happen" question because the underlying fear is that the person would end up dead. It is a question of survival according to the OPD. While these conclusions are not necessarily true, to a child, they are terrifying. A child naturally takes the worst possible outcome and makes it a viable possibility in order to protect herself from it.

Another common fear is abandonment. If a small child is abandoned and no other adult finds them and cares for them, they will die. That fear doesn't just naturally leave when the child grows up and is able to care for himself. When this person gets into a relationship and the loved one threatens to leave, this fear kicks in and it could become a life or death situation for both the individual and for the person leaving.

Death is the fear behind most over-reactions to stimuli although, this fear is not conscious. It is more of an unknown fear for most people. This fear is quite common and easily stimulated. This fear stays with a person throughout life, and most of the time when we over react, it's based on this unconscious fear of death. Survival feels threatened and Eros takes over. The fear is usually unfounded and from an adult, parental point of view, it is quite a leap from "can't do anything right" to death. Unfortunately, in most people who have destructive habits, there appears to be a lack of an internal parent. It appears that a child is in charge of self-protection and it's running on faulty or outdated information.

    Take the time to challenge your OPD's by moving through this, "what might happen if" process with each one. At the same time, keep in your awareness the urgency to lovingly parent the frightened child inside you.

PART THREE:

Change

You've done the hard part. Now here's how to move forward.

Self-Parent to Child Conversations

When a child comes to a caring adult with fears, the adult comforts the child with truthful, yet calming information as well as with affection. The child often doesn't understand new information that counters existing OPD's, but if they feel cared for and if they realize they will not be belittled, they will ask questions. Some of my conversations were as follows:

Inner Child (IC): I can't do anything right
Adult (A): What is right? I just do and if it is not to my liking, I do it again a little different until it is to my liking.

IC: But what if people don't like it?
A: What other people think is none of your concern anyway. What you think of yourself is what matters. That's the only thing you have control over. You can't make someone like you.

IC: But what if it's someone important? Like a boss?
A: In those cases you need to find out what they want from you and determine if it is something you are willing to do. You could learn new skills or you may learn that what they want is unethical. Is the paycheck worth what they want from you?

IC: What if they fire me?
A: I choose to think if I get fired, it means something better is out there. Perhaps it was a job for which my talents were not suited. If you got a job as a first mate on a fishing boat, with your tendency to get sea sick, it might not be a great match.

IC: What if nothing is a good match?

A: I bet if we sit down and write out your interests, we could find a good match. Anything takes practice to get good at it, but many employers know this and as long as you're willing to learn and you're dependable you will do fine. The trick is to find work that complements your passion. Do what you must to make a living, but always work towards an occupation that complements your passion.

IC: I have no place that I belong.

A: You belong where ever you are. You are part of the Universe and belong in it, wherever you are.

IC: I always feel so out of place though.

A: That is only because of what you tend to tell yourself about you. Tell me, what do you tell yourself when you feel out of place?

IC: People will laugh at me. If they got to know me, they would hate me. I can't let them know me. They are the enemy.

A: There are people in the world who, by laughing and conspiring against others, feed their own OPD's. When you allow yourself to be who you are and you change your OPD's, you will feel compassion for those people who laugh and conspire. They will want to belong to your circle of friends

No matter what arguments your inner child comes up with, the loving parent you are developing inside of you can counter it. If you struggle, think of what your **Higher Power** might say to you. If you get stuck, ask someone who you consider to be a loving parent or perhaps ask someone from the clergy. Ask a number of people until you come up with loving answers to your **Inner Child's** fears and OPD's. I suggest you record these conversations on paper or on a digital recorder and keep rereading or listening to them for a while. From these conversations, you will create your own affirmations.

Creating Your Own Affirmations

By comforting yourself in the voice of your **Perfect Parent** and challenging your OPD's, you are in effect saying affirmations similar to the ones mentioned earlier in this book to expose our OPD's. These affirmations are corrections to the OPD's you have been reciting most of your life. This self-abuse has many years of practice. It has become a habit, second nature. Your OPD's are an automatic reaction, triggered without thinking, like driving a car or walking.

Once we learn any of these behaviors, through repetition they become automatic and if we did think about them, we wouldn't do them as well. Stand up, think about how to walk and then do it as you are thinking about it. Break it down into parts and body mechanics, as you probably did as a child. It's not as easy as when you just get up and walk automatically.

Remember that your OPD's were designed to protect you. This system of protection does not understand that it has become outdated and runs on faulty information. The purpose of this technique is to update your protection system so that you may live more fully, without the destructiveness to your happiness. These affirmations act as your point of entry into a life of happiness more times than not. Remember that short affirmations work best.

Here are examples of affirmations I created to counter my OPD's after I wrote my conversations as above:

OPD: *I'm incapable of doing anything right.*
    Affirmations:
- I am capable of doing anything I choose to do.
- If I make a mistake, I choose to correct it and learn from it.
- If what I do is not done as I would like, I may choose to do it again differently.

OPD: *I'm worthless.*
  Affirmations:
- I am a valuable human being
- I decide how valuable I am.
- My value is equal to anyone's.

OPD: *Trust no one.*
  Affirmations:
- I can trust my instincts about people.
- I trust myself to protect myself.
- I entrust my life to my **Higher Power**
- I trust each person I know to be as they are.

OPD: *I'm unlovable*
  Affirmations:
- I am love, thus I am lovable.
- I feel love by releasing it. I can choose that at any time.
- I love myself unconditionally.

OPD: *No one will like me if they know me*
  Affirmations:
- As I learn to like myself, so others will like me.
- If someone chooses to not like me because of who I am, that's their OPD's at work, nothing to do with me.
- Anyone who loves themselves would love me.

These examples have helped me with my OPD's. Create your own affirmations that feel both comforting and loving to yourself as well as to others. Write anything you would have wanted your parents to have said to you. Develop a list of affirmations for your most destructive OPD's and write them out on paper.

PART FOUR:

Reprogramming Yourself

In your life thus far, you have been programmed by society and by your ancestors. They had their own OPD's, some of which you probably inherited. You created quite a few of your own as well. TV, radio, magazines and film add a few more, especially about defining our value in terms of our appearance and possessions. "Humorous" greeting cards plant new or reinforce existing OPD's about aging. Popular put-downs and self-deprecating phrases like, "Duh!" and "I'm having an Alzheimer's moment" sink into the psyche and reinforce OPD's like, "I'm stupid." Or "I'm getting old and therefore less valuable."

With our new affirmations, we now get to *de*-program as well as *re*-program ourselves. Once your OPD's have been identified, challenged and changed, the repetition of the new affirmations will be critical to disarming your triggers.

Practice the new affirmations you created every day, more often is better. When you're alone, say them aloud. Repeat them while driving. Do this for at least twenty-one days. New OPD's may be exposed as you engage in this reprogramming. They may come up more readily and with more force. Your old, outdated protective mechanism is trying to maintain control and get you back in line with what it thinks is in your best interests. Do not buy into the OPD's. When they are at their loudest and cruelest, it means they feel threatened and that you are on the verge of important change. They will soon lose their power and the truth will take hold. Continue exposing your OPD's (by writing them down), challenging them, changing them and reprogramming yourself.

Your OPD's have had years of practice and have become automatic. It doesn't take years to reprogram yourself though, because the affirmations you use to reprogram yourself are the truth. A part of you will know and recognize this, and you will take to it relatively quickly. The only reason it doesn't happen overnight is because you have based your whole life on lies, so it takes a little time to adjust to the idea that life could be any other way than it has been.

The realization that we've been living a lie (even one designed for our survival) can feel overwhelming. You may feel yourself struggling to accept the good things - the truth - about yourself. You may feel drawn to continue living in complexity and turmoil rather than make these changes. If you're aware of this possible reaction, you'll be better able to move through it to happiness.

A FINAL WORD

Because they work best in stealth, just beneath your awareness, your old, outworn, destructive, incorrect beliefs, (OPD's) will lose their power through your newly developed ability to recognize them. The best way to know when an OPD has been triggered is through your body. You will begin feeling that flight or flight feeling - perhaps as a knot in your stomach, or as a headache, or as a shortness of breath – you'll recognize it! *That* is your indication that your OPD's are attempting to exert their power over you via an attack, exposing themselves. Remember, the OPD is not really attacking you because your unconscious mind only knows what it has been programmed to know. It thinks it is protecting you. The purpose of this entire process of *Unconditional Love* is to reprogram your unconscious mind so it may live in the moment and do its job of protecting you using the correct, updated information.

Your recovery consists of daily self-parenting and repetition of your new affirmations (beliefs), combined with your awareness that, until now, your OPD's have been complicating your life and thoughts.

The steps in *Freeing Unconditional Love: Unchaining Your True Self* teach you to depend upon yourself to relate to family, friends and work associates in a more mature manner. When conflicts arise now, you will be able to use this process automatically, stay in the moment and act accordingly. You will be able to see when others are indulging their OPD's and you will know that nastiness or rudeness has nothing to do with you or the present moment.

There will be people who choose to stay in their self-imposed misery, to not do the work as outlined in this book. That is no problem as long as they understand it is a choice and that they may make another choice if and when they desire to do so. The work is quite simple and harmless. There is no reason to continue in misery any longer. Make a commitment to yourself and learn to love yourself unconditionally. The rewards will be that joyous feeling of love, ongoing, beyond your wildest dreams, with no fears of it being taken from you. No one can take it from you. It is one of the very few things over which you do have complete control.

Please send me your stories. I'd love to share them with others as you return to the wonderful being you've always been, free of the negative noise of the OPD's inside. Welcome home.

INDEX

Destructive Thinking Questionnaire

General:
1. Do you entertain your OPD's with any regularity? How often? How much?
2. Do you entertain OPD's to have fun, to socialize, to just be comfortable around people? To fit in? (For example, oftentimes, a group of people will have a discussion about the sad state of affairs in the world, at a job or about health problems. It seems almost socially expected to join in and feed the fear.)
3. Have you ever had any negative consequences from your OPD's and/or related behaviors? List them.
4. What OPD do you find yourself practically enjoying and entertaining the most?
5. People often find certain times or places where they entertain their OPD's with more gusto. Where and when do you prefer to sit and entertain your OPD's?
6. How do you think your OPD's typically affect your behavior?
7. How do you think your OPD's affect you psychologically?
8. How do you think your OPD's affect your loved ones?
9. How do you think your OPD's affect your quality of life?

Food:
10. If you are overweight, how do you think your OPD's contributed?
11. If you are underweight, how do you think your OPD's contributed?
12. How do you think your OPD's prevented you from reaching and/or maintaining your goal weight?
13. How do you think your OPD's affect your choice of foods?

14. How do you think your OPD's affect your eating style (speed of eating, shoveling, picking…)?
15. What other ways do you think your OPD's affect food and nutrition in your life?

Finance:
16. How much money do you spend weekly on destructive habits stemming from your OPD's? (Destructive habits always stem from your OPD's)
17. How much money have you spent as a consequence of entertaining your OPD's?
18. In what ways are you financially liable because of your OPD's? (Debt)
19. In what other ways do you think your OPD's affect your finances and your relationship with money?

Fitness:
20. How do you think your OPD's affect your motivation for exercise?
21. How do you think your OPD's prevent you from making your fitness goals?
22. Have you ever entertained your OPD's while exercising, resulting in injury? Describe.
23. Have you ever cut short a workout due to entertaining your OPD's?
24. In what other ways do you think your OPD's affected your fitness?

Body Care and Hygiene:
25. Do you listen to your OPD's and neglect your teeth? How?
26. How do you think your daily hygiene is influenced by your OPD's?
27. In what other ways do you think your OPD's affect your body care and hygiene?

Work/Vocation/Career:
28. How do you think your OPD's affect your work

performance?
29. How do you think your OPD's affect your ability to maintain work responsibilities?
30. Do you believe you must entertain your OPD's to perform your job? (Do you think that you require the fight or flight response in order to function optimally, to give you an edge)? Explain.
31. Do you think your OPD's and/or related behaviors affect your relationships with customers? Coworkers? Bosses? How?
32. In what other ways do you think your OPD's affect your work/vocation?

Time Management:
33. How does entertaining your OPD's take priority in your schedule?
34. Are some important activities neglected because of your OPD's? Which ones?
35. Are you often late for appointments and meetings or incredibly early because of your OPD's? Explain.
36. Do you tend to get flustered with your time schedule and spend the time entertaining your OPD's instead?
37. In what other ways do you think your OPD's affect your time management?

Leisure/Hobbies:
38. Do you find that the only way to enjoy yourself is by entertaining your OPD's first? Describe.
39. How do you think your OPD's take away from your pleasure in life?
40. Which favorite activities do you no longer enjoy because of your OPD's?
41. In what other ways do you think your OPD's affect your hobbies and leisure?

Spirituality/Religion:
42. Do you believe in spirituality? Have you ever? If there has been a change, what happened?

43. What form does your religion/spiritual life take now?
44. In what ways do you think your OPD's have interrupted your spiritual practice?
45. In what ways do you think your OPD's and/or related behaviors conflict with your spiritual beliefs?
46. In what ways have your OPD's become your God?
47. In what other ways do you think your OPD's have affected your spirituality?

Health:
48. Do you have any health problems? If so, explain.
49. In what ways do you suspect or know your OPD's and related behaviors have affected your health?
50. Do you have aches or pains that you worry are a result of your OPD's and related behaviors? Describe.
51. In what other ways do you think your OPD's affected your health?

Socializing:
52. Have most of your healthy and positive thinking friends dropped out of your life for any reason? If so, please explain.
53. Do the people with whom you spend your time encourage your OPD's? What percent?
54. Do you feel secretive with positive thinking friends or others about your OPD's?
55. Do you tend to feel isolated from the kind of people you would prefer to be around?
56. In what other ways do you think your OPD's are affecting your friendships/social life?

Sexuality:
57. How do you think your OPD's have affected your desire?
58. How do you think your OPD's have affected your sexual performance?
59. How have your OPD's affected your ability to make safe choices in your sexual activities?

60. Have you had any sexual consequences because of your OPD's and related behaviors? Describe.
61. In what other ways do you think your OPD's have affected your sexuality?

Romance:
62. If you have partner, how long have you been together?
63. Do you argue with your partner as a result of your OPD's?
64. Do you sometimes think that it's your partner's fault that you entertain your OPD's? Why?
65. Do you find you would rather spend time entertaining your OPD's and related behaviors than with your partner?
66. Have you ever lost a partner because of your OPD's? How many? Briefly describe the incident(s).
67. Do you fear losing your current partner because of your OPD's? Explain.
68. Have you ever been an embarrassment to your partner because of your OPD's? Describe.
69. How many partners have you gone through because of your OPD's?
70. Do you have trouble finding potential romantic partners? Partners you really desire?
71. How do your OPD's create dissatisfaction with the types of partners you attract?
72. Do you avoid romantic relationships due to your OPD's? What do they say?
73. In what other ways do your OPD's affect your romantic relationships?

Parents:
74. Are your parents still living? If not, how old were you when they died?
75. Are they still together? Or when did they divorce?
76. What are their names and where do/did they live? How old are they/would they be?
77. Have you ever avoided your parents because of your OPD's?

78. Have you ever lied to your parents because of your OPD's?
79. Have you missed many important family gatherings or events because of your OPD's? Which events?
80. Have you ever been an embarrassment to your parents because of your OPD's and related behaviors? Describe.
81. Do you feel bad because you took up the same or similar OPD's or related behaviors as a parent when you swore you'd never be like them?
82. In what other ways do you think your OPD's have affected your relationships with your parents?

Siblings:
83. List the names, ages and locations of your siblings.
84. Are any of your siblings deceased?
85. Have you ever avoided any of your siblings because of your OPD's?
86. Have you ever lied to any of your siblings because of your OPD's?
87. Have you missed or were not invited to important events in your siblings' lives because of your OPD's or related behaviors? Explain.
88. Have you ever thought or been told that you were an embarrassment to your siblings because of your OPD's and related behaviors? Describe.
89. In what other ways do you think your OPD's have affected your relationships with your siblings?

Children/Pets:
90. List the names and ages of your children.
91. Have you ever neglected or even abused your child(ren) because of your OPD's? Describe.
92. Have you ever felt that your children were getting in the way of your OPD's and related behaviors? How?
93. Have you gone out of your way to care for your child, making sure they did not know about your OPD's or related behaviors, only to find that they are still unhappy and/or strangers to you?

94. Have any of your children begun indulging in familiar OPD's or related behaviors of their own? Describe.
95. Have your relationships with your children suffered because of your OPD's? How?
96. If you don't have children, are your pets indifferent or even hostile to you because of your OPD's?
97. Have you ever neglected your pets because of your OPD's? Describe.
98. In what other ways do you think your OPD's have affected your relationships with your children or pets?

Friends/Acquaintances/Perceived Enemies:
99. Do you attract the same kinds of friends all the time?
100. Is there a pattern in your friendships? Do you invite the friendship, does the other person, or is it mutual?
101. Have you ever ended a friendship? If so, have you done it openly or indirectly?
102. Are there any patterns in the kinds of acquaintances you have, or in the types of behaviors that prevent them from becoming friends?
103. How many enemies do you have right now? How have they become enemies?
104. What OPD's are involved in your patterns and choices?

Bosses/Coworkers
105. What kinds of patterns do you notice in the bosses you've had?
106. Make a list of the reasons you left your various jobs. Do you see any patterns?
107. What have your issues been with coworkers?
108. What's your pattern on the job? What role do you fall into?
109. What OPD's are involved in your work relationships?

One important life area I add to this questionnaire is past

traumas. I have found a large number of people in society who have experienced some form of trauma, such as auto accidents, child abuse, witnessing abuse, crime "Victims," war veterans and any other types of accidents. These types of experiences greatly trigger the life force and bring many OPD's into formation. Some of the conclusions are accurate, such as, after an auto accident as a result of driving while distracted with the radio or cell phone, a person might decide to preset the radio stations and only change stations at stop lights or to pull over before using the cell phone. Many people generalize and might refuse to drive or they might blame and berate themselves, unwilling and/or unable to move on and learn from the accident. Some might feel great guilt for surviving a trauma when others may have died.

Past Traumas:
110. List your traumas (violence, abuse, crime, accidents, war, etc.).
111. What do your trauma OPD's tell you when they get triggered?
112. What do your OPD's tell you when you think about your traumas?
113. What do your OPD's tell you when you attempt to talk about your traumas?
114. What do or have your OPD's told you when you attempted to talk about your traumas, but the other person was not able to understand or reacted unfavorably?
115. What typically triggers your trauma OPD's? Make a list.

HEALTHY ALTERNATIVES

Directions

1. Choose the first area of life you want to change and call it area #1. I would recommend that you start with what feels like the least scary area so you can enjoy initial success that will set the tone for the rest of this process. Some people like to go for the scariest first. The choice is yours.
2. Begin incorporating the new behaviors on a daily basis until you have identified the OPD's you think are responsible in this area and you feel comfortable enough to tackle the next area. Apply new behaviors in the second area while you continue practicing area #1. If that is too much, just do one area at a time and don't worry about areas you just finished.
3. Continue this process with other areas until you have your list of OPD's. Take your time and be kind to yourself while you're doing this important work. This is something that you may come back to. There might be OPD's you miss the first time around.
4. Complete each area of change daily until you feel you've mastered the skills. Only then will you truly be able to choose whether you want to utilize the new way or go back to an old way. It's all about choices.
5. Some life areas will appear to be in working order. If so, you decide if you want to apply this process. Sometimes by attempting an area that you feel you have already mastered, by utilizing new choices, you may find a new approach works even better. This will open all sorts of possibilities for you as you realize that perhaps your approaches to life up until now have not been as efficient as they might have been or you might discover that you have a wonderful approach that you could share with others.

6. You will discover layers and layers of OPD's in this process. Write them down. This is a crucial step in exposure
7. Define any words that are not concrete (i.e., love, hate, stupid, smart, etc.) Many people assume they know what a word means, but different people have different definitions of abstract words. The more aware you become of your own definitions, the more likely you will expose your OPD's. By remaining vague, you miss them.
8. Review your OPD Journal each week and identify which beliefs are destructive or counter to your self-enhancement.
9. OPD's will sound logical and try to convince you, using your own logic, why change is not needed or why it is hurtful. Don't listen. None of the alternatives listed in the appendix are dangerous. Use common sense and get a support person to talk to about your fears. OPD's instigate the flight or fight response in response to this approach. The thoughts may come in the form of yelling in your mind with reasons why you should not do this or that alternative behavior.

Food:
1. Inventory all the food in your kitchen. Throw out excess simple carbohydrate foods (cakes, candy, junk foods). Discuss or write about your beliefs about your "blowing it" foods and your beliefs about how various foods affect your body and mind.
2. Complete a meal plan for one day, for one week, and for one month. Follow your meal plan, log all slips and thoughts of resistance. A meal plan simply lists the foods you plan to eat for each meal on any given day. For questions about how to create healthy meal plans, contact a nutritionist, the American Diabetic Association, Weight Watchers, or a group of Overeaters Anonymous who might be able to guide you.

3. Complete a shopping list from your weekly meal plan. If you need guidance, ask advice from mothers or fathers who do the shopping for their families on how to most economically shop at your grocery store of choice. Discuss any resistance with a support person and write beliefs all throughout this process. Your resistance will tell on the OPD's.

Finance:
1. Develop a budgeting plan. Start with listing all monthly income and then all monthly bills, all other bills and other projected spending. Include entertainment as well as more practical spending. Collect all receipts and keep track of all of your spending to compare against your budget.
2. To get out of debt, make monthly payments above the minimum. If you have more than one card, choose one to pay above the minimum and the rest just the minimum. When the first card is paid off, pay above the minimum on the next card. If in severe debt, find an agency like a non-profit Consumer Credit Counseling Service that does this for the public.

Follow the plan and log OPD's:
1. Write about your financial history and history of self-sufficiency. Note which OPD's appear.
2. Define financial success and failure and then look at your actions. Note the differences and similarities.

Fitness:
1. List your beliefs about health, laziness, body image and exercise. What might happen if you looked and felt great?
2. Start a sensible exercise program. No more than an hour a day and no less than 30 minutes. Something aerobic like brisk walking or swimming is great to start. Set your goals and keep a journal. If resistance or slacking off occurs, as in with any area, OPD's are

exposing themselves. Capture them on paper.
3. Continue this process until you are doing at least 30 minutes of aerobic exercise at least 3x per week minimum.
4. When you feel ready, you might want to add stretching or yoga and slowly add weightlifting for toning the muscles. If you have never used weights, either find a personal trainer or buy a good book in order to learn correct form. This will prevent injury.

Body Care and Hygiene:
1. Develop a daily hygiene plan that includes teeth, hair, skin, bathing, clothing and grooming.
2. Write down the OPD's that you have regarding any lapses in this area.
3. Write down the OPD's that say you deserve the punishment of self-neglect.
4. Work at improvement daily. Capture any OPD's that come up.

Work/Vocation/Career:
1. Write your beliefs about your abilities, disabilities (real or perceived), ideals, fears, money, image, worth, and anything else you deem relevant.
2. Describe how you think your OPD's and/or related behaviors affect your relationships with customers? Coworkers? Bosses? How?
3. For each long-term goal, write at least three short-term goals that will assist you in achieving your long-term goals.
4. Begin to follow your plan for accomplishing these goals.
5. If you are under-employed, job hop or are self-employed but failing because of your self-destructive habit(s), document these self-sabotage behaviors each day and develop a plan for substituting new self-enhancing behaviors.
6. Capture any OPD's that appear during this process.

7. In what other ways do you think your OPD's affect your work/vocation?

Time Management:
1. How does entertaining your OPD's take priority in your schedule?
2. Are some important activities neglected because of your OPD's? Which ones?
3. Are you often late for appointments and meetings or incredibly early because of your OPD's? Explain.
4. Do you tend to get flustered with your time schedule and spend the time entertaining your OPD's instead?
5. Create a 168-Hour Weekly Form. On a piece of paper, make seven columns, one for each day of the week. Down the side, on each line, start with midnight on the first line and on the next line, 12:30 am, the next, 1:00 am and so on down the page until you get to 11:30 pm. This will require two pages of 8x11 paper or one page of legal size paper.
6. Make copies of the form or complete it on a computer.
7. For one week, keep a log of how you use your time. Account for all 168 hours. Categories might include: sleep, eating, work, exercise, family, entertainment, hobbies, errands, recovery, friends, crises. Create categories that describe your life and be as specific as possible.
8. At the end of the week, review your log and the way you spend your time. Note how much time has been unaccounted for.
9. Create a 168 Hour Plan for the best use of your time. Most people with destructive habits are crisis-oriented and will benefit from making a schedule and tracking their compliance.
10. Continue to log your time for a month or as long as OPD's are affecting your time management or you feel resistance to this exercise.
11. Let go of any need for perfection. Time management

takes a lot of practice, trial and error and I have found many OPD's instigating the flight or fight response in response to this approach. The thoughts may come in the form of yelling in your mind with reasons why you should not do this scheduling. It will go against possible images you have of yourself of being a *"free"* person, not tied to schedules, etc. Remember, this and all the exercises are temporary unless you later find them advantageous or enjoyable.
12. If you have a tendency to be overly rigid with your time management, I suggest that one or two days a week, you do something spontaneous. Don't plan it. Just look for opportunities as they come up and go for it. It might be friends inviting you to play miniature golf or deciding to do something at a different time than when you usually do it.
13. In what other ways do you think your OPD's affect your time management?

Leisure /Hobbies:
1. Discuss and uncover your beliefs about why you don't deserve to enjoy things you used to enjoy.
2. Come up with a plan for restarting some leisure activities you're no longer doing or for beginning some new ones.
3. Take the first step in your plan. Notice any OPD's that come up.
4. Continue to implement your plan and capture your OPD's as they appear. Some may have to do with keeping a commitment to yourself; some may have to do with leisure and pleasure or why they think you don't deserve it or why it is dangerous such as, "If you have fun or enjoy yourself, since you don't deserve it, you will pay dearly for it." While these are not true, if you don't expose them, many people wind up punishing themselves to prove their OPD's correct. This is a choice and also needs to be exposed.

Spirituality/Religion:
1. List your beliefs and your ideas of *Deity*. Discuss with a support person and write about your theories of how you believe things work in the world and why. Come up with a viable theory, a system or adopt one that you can live with and utilize it daily. A ***Deity*** or a "***Higher Power***" doesn't have to be a "God". Just a power greater than yourself.
2. Come up with a plan for surrounding yourself with positive, spiritual people, writings, and ideas, even if you find them uncomfortable. Attend places of worship other than one you enjoy, ones that really irritate you or that you find distasteful. If you are Christian, attend a temple or a mosque, simply for exposure to other religions and to bring up your OPD's. Many people find strong flight or fight responses regarding religion in response to their OPD's.
3. Uncover and list OPD's daily as they come up.

Health:
1. Write about your main destructive health habit and then any others, from the past or the present that you can identify.
2. Capture the OPD's that come up as you ponder the damage you are doing or that you may have done to your body.
3. List your other destructive health habits from most destructive to least. Capture any OPD's that come up.
4. Make an appointment with a doctor, homeopath or naturopath for a full physical and tell her all your destructive habits. Ask for and listen to her suggestions, then listen to your OPD's to expose them.

Socializing:
1. How comfortable are you in crowds? Do you introduce yourself to others or wait to be introduced? Get invited

to a new social situation and if you tend to wait to be introduced, walk up to everyone you don't know and introduce yourself. If you tend to be the outgoing type, force yourself to wait for others to introduce themselves to you. Write your thoughts about the experience. I suggest doing this exercise a few times.
2. What role do you play in groups? Leader? Follower? Peacemaker? Cheerleader? Rabble-Rouser? Begin purposely playing different roles.
3. Do you prefer to spend time alone?
4. If you prefer alone time, make plans to go to a party or an event such as a block party or a festival. Volunteer for big brothers/sisters and/or join a social club. Pay attention to and then list OPD's
5. Join Toastmasters to learn public speaking. As you begin to make speeches, note your OPD's that expose themselves before, during and after your speech.
6. Start inviting acquaintances or coworkers out to a movie or to lunch. Be honest and let them know you are learning how to socialize better or how to make friends or whatever you find is difficult for you. Most people are honored that you chose them to assist you and will rise to the occasion. If you pick someone who becomes irritated or teases you, take the focus off of them and pay attention to the OPD's they trigger.
7. If you prefer not being alone, arrange time to spend alone doing nothing. Pay attention to your thoughts and feelings.
8. List any OPD's that emerge.

Sexuality:
1. Write about your first sexual experience. How did this affect your beliefs about sex? List any OPD's.
2. Write about your secret beliefs about sexuality, social taboos or deviations from mainstream sexual practices.
3. Write about any experiences of sexual abuse. How have these incidents affected your current sexual

beliefs and practices?
4. What is the most satisfying aspect of your sexuality today? What is least satisfying?
5. Many people say that they feel comfortable with their sexuality. Sometimes they think they are comfortable, but as they talk about it, they feel flight or fight chemicals in their body or OPD's are quietly berating them, chipping away at their defenses. Pay attention to your body and be honest with yourself regarding your body signals and your OPD's.
6. The next time you have sex, list any OPD's that emerge, as soon as possible.
7. The next time you think about making advances toward a sex partner, pay attention to your OPD's. The next time you make the overture to a possible partner, if they decline, capture your OPD's on paper. Do the same if overtures are made toward you, wanted or unwanted.

Romance:
1. How easily do you attract romantic partners or dates? What are your OPD's pertaining to this.
2. Do you ever manipulate your partner? Describe.
3. Write about your fears of intimacy. How willing are you to communicate problems or irritations with a partner? How often do you take responsibility for your own reactions to their behaviors.
4. Do you tend to be the one to leave or be left? Make a list of all your major partners and tally how many you left and how many left you. Capture OPD's along the way.
5. How does it feel to imagine spending the rest of your life alone?
6. How does it feel to imagine spending the rest of your life with a partner?
7. Do you have repetitive arguments with your partner or other family members? Describe on paper how they

typically sound and what usually happens. There are many OPD's that can be found in these arguments. The repetitive nature is the sign of OPD activity.

Parents:
1. List and discuss beliefs about what a perfect parent would act like.
2. How might you have turned out if raised by a perfect?
3. What can you do to parent yourself so you can make your life the way you want?
4. What story about your family or your past might you want to change?
5. Discuss the roles and power you have given your parents and to your self.
6. List things your parent(s) do or did that "Makes you Crazy."
7. List all OPD's that come up during the process.

Siblings:
1. List the similarities you have with your siblings.
2. List the differences.
3. Do you have issues with siblings or their spouses? List.
4. How are you similar and how are you different from your sibling's spouses?
5. Do your siblings ever exclude you in some way? List the OPD's that come up when you think about this.
6. If/when your parents have died, what kind of relationship do you want with your siblings?
7. Create a plan for mending any sort of rift with your siblings. Include short and long term goals, taking into account what you want and what you imagine is their experience with you. It is sometimes easier to just say forget it, but it is not helpful to you or in discovering your OPD's. Family has an uncanny way of triggering our OPD's.

Children/Pets:
1. How many children did you expect to have? How has your reality differed from your plan?
2. Write about and discuss the OPD's that come up when you think about how you may have neglected or abused your children (or pets).
3. Talk about what or who your children represent for you in your life. How do they trigger your OPD's and what are they? Children are often excellent triggers in exposing our OPD's. You will find many in your dealings with your children.

Friends/Acquaintances/Perceived Enemies:
1. Write and discuss OPD's about why you do or don't deserve to have friends or why you don't deserve positive, supportive, caring friends.
2. Is there anyone you find uncomfortable to be around? Write about what OPD's they bring up for you.
3. Devise a plan for mending rifts and making amends to all old friends. Write about and discuss OPD's that come up during this process. In making amends, it's about taking responsibility for your own behaviors, not bringing up their responsibility. You may feel like you're eating crow so to speak. Capture your OPD's on paper.

Bosses/Coworkers:
1. Work is often a microcosm of the family. The boss plays the role of parent. Coworkers and supervisors become siblings. Work is a common place where we reenact their own family dynamics and to continue our behaviors that result from our OPD's. Begin paying attention to this phenomenon and write about you how your work environment is famil(y)iar.
2. Have you ever been fired? For what reasons? What OPD's came up?

3. Do you tend to job hop? For what reasons do you quit jobs? What were the OPD's behind your deciding to quit? How many jobs have you had?
4. If you currently have a problem or resentment toward a boss, coworker, supervisor or a customer, make a plan to make amends and follow through. Capture your OPD's.

Traumas:
1. IF the trauma is scary for you, find a counselor who is trained in **Emotional Freedom Technique** from the website **www.emofree.com**) the **Tearless Trauma Technique** or learn it yourself from the website.

OR

2. Tape record yourself talking about your trauma experience from beginning to end, over and over again. If you don't remember it, start with what you do remember or what you are able to piece together. As you do this, take the role of an emotionless reporter. An observer. This will help in minimizing any flight or fight reactions. When the tape Runs out, rewind and listen to it. Then repeat the process a few times.
3. Many OPD's will make themselves known at just the suggestion of talking about traumas that up till this point may have been silent or disguised except in your unconscious mind. Simply list them and continue the process. Realize the OPD's are lies. The past cannot harm you and neither can the accompanying feelings if you do not resist them.
4. Find a person whom you instruct to listen and not offer advice or comment. Just someone to listen as you repeat the process as with the tape recorder.
5. As you continue this process, you will begin to experience a familiarity in talking about your trauma. Throughout this process, you or your listener may

notice how your story changes as new details come to light. Repetition in talking about traumas is a natural way in which people begin to process and heal traumas. OPD's may tell you you'll die or you will be rejected if you talk about the trauma. Quite the opposite is true. I have known many people who committed suicide years after a trauma if they haven't been able to process the experience adequately through talking about it. Survivor's guilt takes lives and remember, guilt or blame is useless. Even if you feel you had some responsibility for someone's passing, you learn from it, but punishing yourself won't bring back the dead. If your OPD's are unbearable and terrorize you, reach out for assistance in processing your trauma. Vietnam Vet Centers are expert in dealing with Post Traumatic Symptoms. If you are not a Vet, they may help you or give you a qualified referral

Susan Marion

Susan Ann Marion earned a Master's degree in Rehabilitation Counseling from the University of Arizona in 1987. She has 15 years experience in the profession of counseling. with adolescents, adults, people who suffer from all forms of mental illness, all forms of addictions or destructive habits and from all socio-economic levels. She Authored a book in 1989, *A Blueprint for Functional Living: Teaching the 12 Steps to the Dually Diagnosed*. This book was published locally and it put the 12 Steps originated by Alcoholics Anonymous into concrete exercises to make them easier to understand. Susan started massage school in late 1999 and became licensed in massage therapy in 2000.

She opened her massage business in 2004 specializing in Ashiatsu Oriental Bar Therapy. **www.deepfeet.com**.

She began study in early 2005 and became certified as a hand analyst in 2006 **www.handanalyst.com**. Susan developed the process of Unconditional Love coaching over the 15 years she was a counselor and this book is the culmination of her experience using it on herself first and then using it to help others with excellent results and many happy clients.

Susan lives in Florida where she enjoys getting to know her family again. Susan loves her work as a massage therapist, hand analyst and wellness coach. Susan uses the hand analysis in her coaching or as a stand alone service. To contact her, email, **FreeingUnconditionalLove@yahoo.com**. Her website for Ashiatsu Oriental Bar Therapy massage is **www.paradisemassagetherapy.com**

www.ingramcontent.com/pod-product-compliance
Lightning Source LLC
Chambersburg PA
CBHW030330080526
44584CB00012B/790